Data

This book explores the phenomenon of data – big and small – in the contemporary digital, informatics, and legal-bureaucratic context.

Challenging the way in which legal interest in data has focused on rights and privacy concerns, this book examines the contestable, multivocal, and multifaceted figure of the contemporary data subject. The book analyses 'data' and 'personal data' as contemporary phenomena, addressing the data realms, such as stores, institutions, systems, and networks, out of which they emerge. It interrogates the role of law, regulation, and governance in structuring both formal and informal definitions of the data subject, and disciplining data subjects through compliance with normative standards of conduct. Focusing on the 'personal' in and of data, the book pursues a re-evaluation of the nature, role, and place of the data subject qua legal subject in on- and offline societies: one that does not begin and end with the inviolability of individual rights but returns to more fundamental legal principles suited to considerations of personhood, such as stewardship, trust, property, and contract.

The book's concern with the production, use, abuse, and alienation of personal data within the context of contemporary communicative capitalism will appeal to scholars and students of law, science and technology studies, and sociology; as well as those with broader political interests in this area.

Robert Herian is a senior lecturer in Law at the Open University. His research covers intersections of law, technology, and data, and he is also the author of *Regulating Blockchain: Critical Perspectives in Law and Technology*, Routledge 2018.

Part of the NEW TRAJECTORIES IN LAW series

Series editors

Adam Gearey, Birkbeck College, University of London
Colin Perrin, Commissioning Editor, Routledge

For information about the series and details of previous and forthcoming titles, see https://www.routledge.com/New-Trajectories-in-Law/book-series/NTL

A GlassHouse Book

Data
New Trajectories in Law

Robert Herian

Routledge
Taylor & Francis Group
a GlassHouse Book

First published 2021
by Routledge
2 Park Square, Milton Park, Abingdon, Oxon OX14 4RN

and by Routledge
605 Third Avenue, New York, NY 10017

A GlassHouse Book

*Routledge is an imprint of the Taylor & Francis Group,
an informa business*

British Library Cataloguing-in-Publication Data

A catalogue record for this book is available from the British Library

Library of Congress Cataloging-in-Publication Data

Names: Herian, Robert, author.
Title: Data: new trajectories in law/Robert Herian.
Description: Milton Park, Abingdon, Oxon; New York, NY:
    Routledge, 2021.
Series: New trajectories in law | Includes bibliographical
    references and index.
Identifiers: LCCN 2020047494 (print) | LCCN 2020047495 (ebook) |
    ISBN 9780367477134 (hardback) | ISBN 9781003162001 (ebook)
Subjects: LCSH: Databases–Law and legislation. | Data protection–Law
    and legislation. | Privacy, Right of.
Classification: LCC K564.C6 H47 2021 (print) | LCC K564.C6 (ebook) |
    DDC 343.09/99–dc23
LC record available at https://lccn.loc.gov/2020047494
LC ebook record available at https://lccn.loc.gov/2020047495

ISBN 13: 978-0-367-47713-4 (hbk)
ISBN 13: 978-0-367-75330-6 (pbk)

Typeset in Times New Roman
by KnowledgeWorks Global Ltd.

Contents

Introduction

To whom it may concern

In the last five years, whilst researching and analysing developments at the intersection of law and distributed ledger technologies (DLTs), blockchains, and smart contracts, I became increasingly interested in the bits, nibbles, and bytes of personal data collected, stored, compounded, and aggregated into information and tied to the utility of DLTs and myriad other software and hardware technologies. These granular accretions of systemic and systematic inputs and outputs, data produced by quantitative and qualitative empiricism, all circulating through platforms, systems and networks and stimulating commodification, commerce, and surveillance in its wake. What particularly caught my attention were dialogues, narratives, bonds, and tensions between the methods and processes of production, storage, and exchange of personal data – of which DLTs and blockchains continue to play an emergent role – and the stakeholder motivations for creating and tapping stores of personal data as a valuable resource, 'fuel' to 'power' today's data-driven societies and economies. Behind these promises in the form of different technological solutions that aim to give 'netizens', consumers, platform users, and network stakeholders, however we choose to view these increasingly hybridised and compounded on- and offline communities, greater transparency, control, self-care, and sovereignty over personal data. But, if the perception is of many private enterprises and increasingly public and civic services and governance bodies needing to give greater control back to individuals or consumers over personal data, a counter narrative asks whether individuals or consumers need, want, or desire this responsibility in return, or, indeed, are even capable of taking control at all.

Following the legal sociology of my previous work on DLTs, in the simplest terms and most convenient definitions, this book aims at something different: a philosophical and phenomenological analysis of personal data, the data subject, and the one to whom personal data relates. My primary aim is not to approach this duality between data and subject anthropocentrically or as a matter of epistemology but of ontology. The discussion that follows concerns human *and* non-human subjects, objects, things, and beings and takes seriously claims that there is vastly more ontological ground than that upon which human beings, alone, stand.[1] The particular focus I have outlined does not preclude discussion of the economic, political, nor, of course, the legal. But, again, I do not view these and will not consider them only of consequence to mankind (anthropos). Similarly, whilst I will not discuss personal data and the data subject as objects hopelessly abstracted from one another or unrelated to technologies for instance, the ways in which they do interrelate with each other and to the technologies that so often define them, especially in the eyes of economics and law, will not be treated as inconsequential and beyond question or reproach (absolute), but as significant tensions and bonds that tell us as much about the autonomy of a thing (its non-relations) as it does about its relations (Harman, 2016).

It is common today for datum to provide the principal basis for all types of reasoning and calculation, and for data and information as pluralised, aggregated and mechanically and technologically processed stages of datum to provide principal sources of instructive knowledge. As with the reform and advance of laws, data (as facts) often marry with reason, in a legacy of enlightenment thinking, in principles of sufficient reason, that Gottfried Leibniz described as why something should be 'thus and not otherwise', although he importantly caveats this 'even though in most cases these reasons cannot be known to us' (1973, p. 184). Personal data thus aims always at describing subjective experiences of the world, the myriad events, practices, contexts, conditions, environments that we desire or need to make sense of, but it always ultimately fails because it can never provide a total picture of things and, accordingly, we cannot know everything irrespective of the volume of reason we apply. Data and information are the ultimate mediators of experience and being in today's world, powerful yet not immutable sources of truth. It has become as easy to check the local weather on a smartphone whilst still in bed in the morning than to get up and look out of the window. And even if we do bother to get up will we believe our eyes if the weather data on our phones does not exactly match what is happening outside? How humanity senses the world has traditionally concerned the collective and combinatory fundamentals of smell, taste, touch, and so on.

Today, with my smartphone ready-at-hand, the individual sensory field widens to encompass proximity, acceleration, orientation, and angular velocity. Whilst surveillance is considered, whether for good or ill, a mark of the Information Age, it is only possible because of the ubiquity of sensors. And yet personal datum (or any data) do not come into existence only because it is sensed or perceived.

Information technology *qua* knowledge industries are vast, powerful, and influential in the twenty-first century but that is not proportionate to the number of sensors they have searching for data. Vast accretions, stores, lakes, and clouds of intermingled personal and non-personal data (so-called 'big data') underpin data operations (DataOps) models and algorithmic predictive pathways and modes of analysis that touch and concern all areas of modern life. 'Big data' totalling zettabytes (10^{21}) has the type of fundamental otherness and conceptual obscurity that only large numbers, immense landscapes, or seemingly infinite space creates in the human mind. Yet reliance on this data by a variety of stakeholders is the foundation of most administrative, organisational, and bureaucratic methods operating globally today. As data subjects, therefore, we daily swim, or perhaps tread-water, in a deep, dark, and forbidding ocean of data that we cannot possibly begin to comprehend. Not because it is nothing to do with us, not 'our' or 'my' data, or because we find it alien or unrelatable at a technological level, but because I, you, or we can never directly know or relate to the data called 'personal'. It escapes and withdraws from us at every turn. More than that, it escapes and withdraws from the methods of processing and organisation – the algorithmic functions – for which it is supposed to deliver meaning and insight. I may look at a pair of jeans on Amazon one week, but when the recommendation for that pair or similar pair of jeans magically appears in my account the next week there is no guarantee I will buy them. My personal data gathered as a preference indicator is wholly probabilistic and, therefore, in the last judgement a poor substitute for certainty, but only because that certainty was never there in the first place.

The lack of knowledge and comprehension of and with personal data, including one's status as a data subject-at-large in the Information Age, does not begin and end with the very big. From the point of view of philosophical and critical discussions of personal (or non-personal) data, 'big data' is not, I argue, a good place to start at all. As a concept, 'big data' is designed to enthral us in the same way that vast expanses of space and distant horizons do. Both can be horrifying or sublime. Equally they present opportunities to those willing to take on the rush, scramble, and risks associated with conquering new territories and mining value in the hope of securing wealth, power, and prestige. Where the latter is concerned, we often find that heroic figure of the neoliberal capitalist age, the entrepreneur, in constant need of data and information to feed the avaricious engine of her 'start-up'. But, of course, demand and hunger for 'big data' transcends private and public interests with all wedded to idea of capitalising on the value of data both financially and in terms of efficiency. By contrast, 'small data' (personal data) and even the larger aggregate, personal information, is not designed to mesmerise but is a mere unit to be consumed and devoured by the greater and glorious 'big'.[2] This makes personal data of marginal or fleeting consequence, if any at all. It is mundane, common, ordinary, and only slight in value, although never quite valueless. Here, however, it is precisely what interests us. This is not another book about the monolithic concept of 'big data'; this is not a book about what 'big data' is but one about what 'big data' are.

Personal data exists not only in a processed and often monetised informatic forms (datafication), but also *prior* to any collation of 'raw' data by automated systems, online platforms, databases, networks, and other repositories of content for the administration, management, discipline, and commodification of individuals and communities that both use and come, inexorably, to rely upon them. Analyses of personal data-as-phenomenon and readings that take the vitality of personal data seriously, such as the one proposed here, turn on personal data as *sourced* and appearing from the being of the 'data subject'. The data subject, whilst a relatively new concept in the *longue durée* of legal subjectivities, is one that has assumed a coherent form and presence, at least in the imagination of UK lawmakers, because of the continued rise from the late 1960s onwards of automated (or 'automatic') methods and systems for capturing, recording and processing personal information and data traceable to identifiable individuals (Durbin, 1979; Regan, 1984; Warren and Dearnley, 2005). As societies in countries around the world have, in both public and private realms, increasingly come to rely on sensors and ambient computing for recording and surveillance of many if not most aspects of social life, the data subjects within those societies have grown in complexity and, as the barer of rights, also in legal stature and significance.

This is not a book solely concerned with the law of privacy or concerns triggered by pervasive private and public computer use. But because concepts, practices, and policies concerning data subjects and personal data exist in lockstep with issues of data privacy and protection it is not possible to avoid the legal matter of privacy. As Warren and Dearnley maintain: 'Data protection legislation in the UK and other European countries stemmed from this growing reliance on collecting personal data, and from the realisation that unfettered collection and distribution of personal documentation and data potentially or placed individual privacy at risk' (2005, p. 239). The data subject is an embodiment of individual human experience in contemporary digitalised societies, the beneficiary of many technological facilities and methods. But data subjects also make up a public long-since anxious about the use and abuse of computerised personal information (Durbin, 1979, p. 302).

The data subject is at once an individual bringer and giver of data and receiver of rights and protections of and over the stuff called 'personal data', where such data is attributable to them as set out within legislation. But the data subject is also one who is often in ignorance, one for whom the status and nature of personal data are at once mysterious and burdensome. Whilst increasingly intimately associated with technologies like smartphones and the technological know-how that accompanies them, data subjects vary in awareness as to their status as sources of personal data or understanding of its value or fate as it circulates within and helps grease the wheels of business and, by extension, global capitalist economies. This book's exploration of data subjects and personal data, whilst still a broad landscape of inquiry, aims to narrow and focus the field of inquiry by discussing human data and the 'data subject' human, rather than including a broader analysis of data collected from machines or non-human entities. What is data? Starting from the questions what personal data is and what is the relationship between personal data and the data subject has led to this book's underlying task: a *phenomenology of personal data*, a task underpinning three further distinct yet interrelated categories of analysis:

1 *Juridical* – including questions of sovereignty, agency, property, and control
2 *Economic and bureaucratic* – including questions of governance, power, efficiency, value, and labour
3 *Psycho-political* – including questions of subjectivity, alienation, and dignity

Against a contemporary backdrop of the extractive and exploitative potentialities embodied by 'big data', notions of 'content' and pervasive 'datafication', the subset and, perhaps, countervailing phenomenon of personal data, as that which is in a constant state of becoming with the data subject ('personal data subject'), warrant attention.

Funnelled through various technologies, personal data straddles the various analyses I highlight above.[3] 'As every man goes through life he fills in a number of forms for the record, each containing a number of questions. A man's answer to one question on one form becomes a little thread', says Alexander Solzhenitsyn in his novel *Cancer Ward,* and 'There are thus hundreds of little threads radiating from every man, millions of threads in all' (2003, p. 208). Reflecting on the image of 'hundreds of little threads radiating from every man' Solzhenitsyn describes, suggests, I argue, personal data as *sourced*, appearing from being. Personal data is at once ephemeral, infinitely expansive, profligate, and the means to identify, verify, and recognise that foreshadows extractive and exploitative potentialities.[4] A phenomenology of data therefore seeks to bring to light (phainō) a sense of the personal data subject as such, as 'that it is', a 'self-showing in itself' that tells us something about the personal data subject before and its entry into the communicative transactional systems and networks of neoliberal capitalism (Heidegger, 2011, pp. 30–32). We might, for example, in a bastardisation of Heidegger, refer to da(ta)sein as means of describing the appearance of data in being, as an authentic articulation of the personal of data and the becoming (legal birth) of the *personal data subject* from the one to whom data relates.

Mantras or clichés such as 'data is the new oil' shared across neoliberal capitalist and, increasingly, alternative market economies (i.e. China) provide obvious and colourful indicators of what is at stake from mass datafication and the proliferation of global data markets (*The Economist*, 2017). As 'oil', data from personal and impersonal sources satisfies duel economic interests within capitalism to maintain a sense of scarcity and proprietary value and thus provides a rationale for data's inclusion in the growth principles and practise of contemporary economies both overtly capitalist and alternative market forms, namely China (Kai-Fu Lee, 2018). Applying a little pressure to the analogy, however, sees it break down. Rarely if ever, for instance, do we hear data or its refined form, information referred to as a pollutant (spilling like oil), although spam and 'fake news' are, arguably, manifestations of this. Nor is the scarcity of data remotely comparable to that of oil, a finite and highly contestable resource. Unlike oil, we do not find personal data in specific locations, countries, or regions such as the North Sea, Venezuela, or the Middle East, but eschews territorialisation. And, to date at least, personal data has not been an explicit cause of major global geo-political tensions or wars, as oil has.[5]

The data/oil analogy cannot describe what is at stake in terms of the personal cost of (un)productivity and, perhaps most tellingly, is silent on digital practices akin to the ritual sacrifice of parts of one's being or bodily integrity, the products of which are data gathered in mass stores or sites of waste. A way of illustrating this view of personal data is via the documentary film *Good Hair* (2009) which looks at the entrepreneurial practice of harvesting black hair from India for markets in African American hair extensions (weaves) in the United States. As the film highlights, those taking part in the ritual of 'tonsure' in India do so willingly in the belief that the shaving of the head is an important sacrifice within the ambit of Hindu scripture but are unaware of where their hair ends up going or how much it is worth. This practice, in many respects, echoes personal data sourcing as a principle of capitalist exploitation. A more abstract notion of personal data 'tonsure', or what Adam Greenfield calls 'shedding traces', describes a whole array of datafication practices within contemporary capitalism (2018, p. 25).

Short of claiming every data subject is akin to a devotee 'farmed' for their data-as-hair (a point the film raises), the interpersonal relationship between the hair giver and wearer or user and those who 'farm', market, and sell describes a transactional dynamic familiar to markets for personal data. It presents an opportunity for rethinking law's understanding of and approaches to datafication, and whether these approaches can be improved or presented with more clarity. The commercial harvesting and sale of hair like other body parts is a regulated industry, and such regulatory standards, whether positive or negative, could feed into new ways of thinking about data and its regulation (Mitchell, 2004; Rai, 2004). For instance, as *Good Hair* portrays it, the farming of devotee's hair is an industry that extracts value deceitfully, by literally sweeping away the commodity (hair) before the ritual ('tonsure') is even complete. Perhaps without this enterprise the hair would perish or rot and collecting it is a form of waste recycling. In contemporary parlance, we might say it creates a 'circular economy' for re-finding value in what is unwanted, left over, or left behind, and the same applies for personal data. A normative legal approach in both instances is to ask who the beneficiaries of the re-found value are and the mechanisms (legal, political, and economic) to establish rights as against former and future owners of the commodity (data or hair). Hence, personal data protections have become solidly rights-based in most jurisdictions, and personal data is seen as a form of private property over which subjects have rights to exclude others, as well as rights to use, abuse, and alienate 'their' data.

Issues and questions of rights and who is, at law, in a position to treat data as property (or commodity), to sell, give, and take data, speak to the wide variety of controls and regulations that now span international jurisdictions, including the European Union's General Data Protection Regulation (GDPR). And whilst the variety of laws and regulations protecting data subjects provide important standards and guidance regarding data handling and management, the outcome of much of the legal reasoning concerned with data protections and privacy is a generic fiction of the data subject and, therefore I argue, an impoverished sense of the relationship between a person (subject) and data derived from their being (personal data) (Blume, 2015, p. 259).

To whom personal data relates

This book's appeal to lawyers (and others) is in its contribution to critical appraisals of the individual, society, and laws that are in a state of becoming and yet to become in the wake of technological development and evolution within capitalism. 'Data subjects' are the individuals in question, the legal subjects at the heart of the global Information Age, the 'you', 'me', and 'them' online. Yet, as this book will show by attempting to get under the skin, so to speak, of this contemporary, individualised and individualising techno-legal phenomenon, data subjectivities describe an *excess* of normative legal certainty or finitude that otherwise renders them identified or identifiable living individuals 'to whom personal data relates' (s.3 *Data Protection Act* 2018 c.12). Law's inherent conservatism and desire to scrutinise context and event in-depth mean it so often trails behind the increasingly rapid leaps and bursts of technological change and struggles to keep pace with innovations happening at the speed of thought.[6] It is perhaps unsurprising, therefore, that attempts in the law of England and Wales to identify and categorise reasonable, rational, liable, consensual, or accountable subjects within the tumult of the capitalist information age produce impoverished and base functional responses. Between the identified individual and the 'to whom personal data relates' are epistemological and ontological gaps growing in size and stature with every new technological shift and innovation.

It is the overarching thesis of this book that the legal fiction of the data subject cannot grasp or suitably represent the relationship between the subject and data. Further, the legal fiction cannot define the "personal" of data in the age of "big" data accretions, storage and transactions within the business models of contemporary digital enterprise. One route to a richer understanding of that relationship, I argue, is through a phenomenology of data. For me, the data subject deserves the same scrutiny that critical legal scholarship and thinking has given to a broad range of subjectivities. The importance of scrutinising the data subject in this way is one I hope to convince normative legal thinking of equally. The need to better understand not only the benefits and concerns surrounding data as a product or commodity but what is at stake in and from generative sources of data, namely data subjects, cannot be underestimated in the networked digital age in which we are all enmeshed. The growth in data brokerage and marketplaces as a fundamental response to the inequities of recent data practices by the likes of Facebook shows that a re-appraisal of the significance of data in and to contemporary societies is well underway in social discourse. As Richard Powers highlights in this passage from his novel, *The Overstory*.

Signals swarm through Mimi's phone. Suppressed updates and smart alerts chime at her. Notifications to flick away. Viral memes and clickable comment wars, millions of unread posts demanding to be ranked. Everyone around her in the park is likewise busy, tapping and swiping, each with a universe in his palm. A massive, crowd-sourced urgency unfolds in Like-Land, and the learners, watching over these humans' shoulders, noting each time a person clicks, begin to see what it might be: people, vanishing en masse into a replicated paradise (2018, p. 597).

The subject of this book is not only useful but also, I modestly argue, important as a theoretical and perhaps above all philosophical contribution to processes of re-thinking, expanding, challenging, and potentially re-shaping legal and broader narratives dealing with data and data subjectivities. As this book will discuss, scholars undertaking critical data studies have been challenging normative thinking and practices around data and data subjectivities for some time – challenging what I refer to as the *datus quo*. Of particular concern here is a replication of the scrutiny by critical data studies – the desire to get under the skin of data and data practices – in law, especially of the data subject and beyond the doctrinal task of defining the data subject at the level of legal accountability within what are, largely, contexts of consumer protection. The data subject is a good example of what Costas Douzinas and Adam Gearey have referred to as the 'cognitive impoverishment' of jurisprudence, because the data subject as we find it is entirely a product of technocratic legalism, 'a science of what – legally – exists, and a legitimation of current policies' (2005, p. 4). It is important to challenge and shift existing legal perspectives, thinking, and narratives on data subjectivity and the practices that thinking informs. To offer a richer account of the data subject released from the clutches of technocratic legalism.

Scope and structure

This is not a long book and despite the thousand ships potentially launched by the introductory outline above there is not the time or space to cover all angles, answer all questions, or address all concerns relating to personal data, data subjects, privacy, and so on. Foremost, as a book rooted in juridical concerns, the main context (jurisdiction) will be the United Kingdom, and specifically the laws of England and Wales ('English law') that speak to the matter of personal data and the data subject. Given that the concepts of the data subject and personal data have not developed solely in the imagination of UK lawmakers, we will also discuss relevant examples from Anglo-American socio-political life and law, notably those from the United States that led the way both in developing and interrogating the power of computerised data from the middle of the last century. We will also discuss the law of the European Union ('EU') and by extension civil law, and the experience of the Scandinavian countries that helped to start many of the debates surrounding data use and abuse on this side of the Atlantic in the mid-twentieth century. The EU's recent data protection and privacy laws in the form of the GDPR, which seem to describe the high-water mark of global data protection standards, is of particular interest here.

This book takes both critical and law in context approaches, hence analysis of the evolution of legal thinking and practice around personal data will involve historical, cultural, political, and economic background in the United Kingdom and beyond, and will do so, broadly, from the latter part of the twentieth century to the present day. What the future will hold is anyone's guess. Where there are clear markers of the direction of national (or international) conventions, practices, and standards on personal data, this book will attempt future-gazing. It is important to note that this book draws, at least in the early stages, on the recent history of data protection and privacy concerns in private and public life. In terms of future developments – where personal data may take us into the first quarter of the twenty-first century – this recent history may provide important lessons. What underlies the claim to history's value is simple but not straightforward. The anxieties, arguments, debates, promises had and made in the public squares of the United States and Britain in the mid-twentieth century, the time of the birth of the data subject as a peculiarly digital, computerised social phenomenon, have not changed a great deal in the intervening sixty years. This despite radical and far-reaching technological changes, such as the Internet. Participants in the debates of the 1960–70s could barely have imagined, let alone conceive of the scale of digital socialisation and participation we see today. Foundational and fundamental principles and concerns raised about privacy and 'date banks' remain, however, at the heart of social unease with personal data use and abuse, data subjectivity, and the formation and maintenance of digital selves.

Chapters 1 and 2 explore the 'datus quo', my deliberate pun on *status quo* and its normative and dominant legal ideas and practices on personal data, including how the 'data subject' became a coherent legal concept, warranting mention in various committees conducted by the UK Parliament from 1970 onwards, and parliamentary debates from 19 December 1980 (HC Deb, vol. 996, col. 704). Further, *datus* in its original form also refers to an act of giving, especially of oneself, that bears heavily on the notion of data discussed in the later chapters of the book. The normative appraisal of personal data and subjectivity established in Chapter 2, therefore, prepares the ground for the critical themes discussed later. Chapter 2 will outline normative perspectives and impressions including contemporary legislative constructions of personal data and the 'data subject',[7] broader cultural narratives concerning individual and/or group control of and sovereignty over personal data, and, importantly, examine how capitalism shapes data via narratives such as 'data is (the new) oil'.

Chapter 3 looks at 'being in data' and asks the question 'what is personal data?' Drawing on Heidegger's phenomenology and, in particular, his work on technology, the chapter will undertake a core aim of the book by outlining data-as-phenomenon, exploring the perception of being animating data that produces perceptions of *dataness* that precede the emergence of the data subject as it exists in contemporary legal thinking and practice. The aim of the chapter is also to establish data as phenomenon *contra* data as right. To bring to light novel ways of viewing the data subject as always already intimately relating to 'their' data prior to rights and regulatory interventions aimed at protecting data subjects. The chapter acts as a keystone between conceptions of rights and the data subject and the alternative conceptions set-out by the book in the following chapters.

Chapter 4 will examine the idea of 'data with subject' in different contexts and from a variety of sources as novel, counter narratives to prevailing legal notions of personal data and data subjectivity. The chapter will focus on the relationship between the subject and data, including the ways and means that contemporary capitalist subjects offer, give, or sacrifice personal data. Following themes introduced above, the chapter will discuss topics such as: shedding data – e.g. the (over) production and consumption of the self as data waste; and data 'tonsure' – ritual, ecstatic, and sacrificial data practices, introducing the idea of data as hair in contradistinction to 'data as oil'. Finally, Chapter 5 will offer conclusions via a discussion of the theme of data in the time of Covid-19.

Notes

1. This claim is central to the philosophical movement known as object-orientated ontology (OOO). This book will discuss the significance of OOO in terms of personal data and data subjectivity at different points throughout, and especially in later chapters.
2. Bits, nibbles, and bytes of data are, of course, all 'edible' metaphors.
3. The contemporary figure of the '(nano)influencer' or 'content creator' is an interesting and, I would argue, deeply cynical manipulation of the 'personal' by private enterprise wanting to extract value from increasingly niche data sources.
4. The function of 'recognition' here is twofold: as a commentary on existence in cyberspace, for example, within the ambit of social media in which content and 'likes' establish recognition; and, following Hegel via Alexander Kojève, recognition as the final function of anthropogenetic desire. The two are, I argue, sides of the same coin. Broadly speaking, the former constitutes a *conscious* striving for recognition, while the latter is *unconscious* (Kojève, 1969, p. 7).
5. Growing tensions between the United States and China over global information infrastructures suggest that data could well begin to imitate oil on this matter very soon, however.
6. Law on patents may be considered the outlier in this regard, in so far as patent protections form the basis of much industrial and commercial strategy and, therefore, technologists or innovators can ill-afford to ignore the need to protect ideas and inventions from possible competitors and reach out to patent attorneys as a matter of urgency.
7. Example of legislative constructions include:
GDPR Article 4 – Definitions
   (1) 'personal data' means any information relating to an identified or identifiable natural person ('data subject'); an identifiable natural person is one who can be identified, directly or indirectly, in particular by reference to an identifier such as a name, an identification number, location data, an online identifier or to one or more factors specific to the physical, physiological, genetic, mental, economic, cultural, or social identity of that natural person
   Data Protection Act 2018 (incorporating GDPR)
   3 Terms relating to the processing of personal data

(1) This section defines some terms used in this Act.

(2) 'Personal data' means any information relating to an identified or identifiable living individual (subject to subsection (14)(c)).

(3) 'Identifiable living individual' means a living individual who can be identified, directly or indirectly, in particular by reference to –

(a) an identifier such as a name, an identification number, location data or an online identifier, or

(b) one or more factors specific to the physical, physiological, genetic, mental, economic, cultural or social identity of the individual.

(4) 'Processing', in relation to information, means an operation or set of operations which is performed on information, or on sets of information, such as—

(a) collection, recording, organisation, structuring or storage,

(b) adaptation or alteration,

(c) retrieval, consultation or use,

(d) disclosure by transmission, dissemination or otherwise making available,

(e) alignment or combination, or

(f) restriction, erasure or destruction, (subject to subsection (14)(c) and sections 5(7), 29(2) and 82(3), which make provision about references to processing in the different Parts of this Act).

(5) 'Data subject' means the identified or identifiable living individual to whom personal data relates.

References

The Economist. 2017. The World's Most Valuable Resource Is No Longer Oil, but Data. https://www.economist.com/leaders/2017/05/06/the-worlds-most-valuable-resource-is-no-longer-oil-but-data (accessed 16 May 2019).

Blume, Peter. 2015. The Data Subject. *European Data Protection Law Review.* Vol. 1, No. 4, pp. 258–264.

Data Protection Act 2018, c.12.

Douzinas, Costas and Adam Gearey. 2005. *Critical Jurisprudence: The Political Philosophy of Justice.* Oxford: Hart.

Durbin, J. 1979. Statistics and the Report of the Data Protection Committee. *Journal of the Royal Statistical Society, Series A.* Vol. 142, No. Part 3, pp. 299–306.

Greenfield, Adam. 2018. *Radical Technologies: The Design of Everyday Life.* London: Verso.

Stilson, Jeff. 2009. *Good Hair.* [Documentary]. USA: HBO Films.

Harman, Graham. 2016. *Immaterialism: Objects and Social Theory.* Cambridge: Polity.

Heidegger, Martin. 2011. *Basic Writings.* Edited by David Farrell Krell. London: Routledge.

Kojève, Alexander. 1969. *Introduction to the Reading of Hegel.* Edited by Allan Bloom. Translated by James H. Nichols, Jr. New York: Basic Books.

Lee, Kai-Fu. 2018. Data Is the New Oil, and China Is the New Saudi Arabia, Says AI Expert. *CNBC*, 24 September. https://www.cnbc.com/video/2018/09/24/data-china-tech-trade-war-artificial-intelligence.html (accessed 7 January 2020).

Leibniz, Gottfried Wilhelm. 1973. *Philosophical Writings*. Edited by G. H. R. Parkinson. London: J.M. Dent & Sons.

Mitchell, Robert. 2004. $ell: Body Wastes, Information, and Commodification. *Data Made Flesh: Embodying Information*. Edited by Robert Mitchell, Phillip Thurtle. New York: Routledge, pp. 121–136.

Powers, Richard. 2018. *The Overstory*. London: Vintage.

Rai, Saritha. 2004. A Religious Tangle Over the Hair of Pious Hindus. *New York Times*, 14 July. https://www.nytimes.com/2004/07/14/world/a-religious-tangle-over-the-hair-of-pious-hindus.html (accessed 6 January 2020).

Regan, Priscilla M. 1984. Personal Information Policies in the United States and Britain: The Dilemma of Implementation Considerations. *Journal of Public Policy*. Vol. 4, No. 1, pp. 19–38.

Solzhenitsyn, Alexander. 2003. *Cancer Ward*. London: Vintage.

Warren, Adam and James Dearnley. 2005. Data Protection Legislation in the United Kingdom: From Development to Statute 1969–84. *Information, Communication & Society*. Vol. 8, No. 2, pp. 238–263.

1 Beautiful machines and bureaucratic dreams

Introduction

The following two chapters explore the recent history and the *status*, or rather, *datus quo* of personal data; the data subject; datafication ideas, policies, and practices; and the laws developed to regulate, govern, and legitimise them, including notable recent examples, the 2016 European Union General Data Protection Regulation (GDPR) and 2018 Californian Consumer Privacy Act (CCPA).[1] My use of the term *datus*, a Latin root of datum, meaning an act of giving, especially of oneself, refers both to the linkages and slippages between ancient Western understanding of the relationship between data and persons (subjectivities encompassing personal data), and the present globalised conceptualisations of data subjectivity written in laws, regulations, and codes.[2] Where we have seen a significant shift in meaning between the contemporary *datum* (and the plural data, which I shall refer to most often during this book) and the ancient *datus*, I argue, concerns today's 'enlightened' interest in reason and calculation as the basis, even the purpose for datum. Capitalism directs an emphasis on reason and calculation to economic ends such as profit and commercial growth, and neoliberal capitalism to promoting the proliferation of markets both big and small and adrenaline-fuelled adventures in games of fiscal risk at individual and corporate levels. Hence, datum is today less a giving oneself than a taking thereof, where the latter represents committed strategies of a range of actors and stakeholders for a variety of purposes, many or most of which have commercial consequences.

Personal and non-personal data inform much of the decision-making in today's world and is, therefore, considered an important and indispensable authority. Broadly, we can define data as known or assumed facts, and when processed and aggregated into information is the basis of instructive knowledge that shapes and steers policies, strategies, and behaviours. In terms of personal data, there are a number of different sub-divisions and sub-definitions that we can make, indeed throughout this book we will uncover news ways of describing and seeing personal data that will demand fresh definition. But for present purposes we can further sub-divide personal data along the lines set-out by Luciano Floridi, which are *'arbitrary* data *about* oneself (e.g. a name and surname)' and *'ontic* data – that is, data *constituting* someone (e.g. someone's DNA), or constituting the *interpretation* of someone as an informational entity' (2013, p. 247). It is no longer the case that public and private organisations, corporations, institutions, charities and, increasingly, individuals can function and interact in the world without some recourse to or acknowledgement of their own data or data relating to others. Societies today reflect data as a necessity for striving to mitigate ignorance, encourage knowledge and understanding, and ensure the victory of truth. To use data analytics is, in this sense, to muster the forces of both truth and common sense. But whilst businesses may view, as common sense, data to improve efficiency and performance, common sense as a broader social directive is itself increasingly made a subset of and product of these data analytical practices.

Data as common sense is akin to a cybernetic feedback loop that, to echo Heidegger, aims at establishment and reinforcement of the obviousness of everything actual (2011). 'Common sense has its own necessity', claims Heidegger, 'it asserts its rights with the weapon particularly suitable to it, namely appeal to the "obviousness" of its claims and considerations' (2011, p. 66). Data has perhaps replaced older or outmoded oracles of virtue, instruction or authority that performed the same role, and there is an interesting correlation between a generalised conception of the function of data and markets. The difference between data, or rather how we use it in contemporary societies, and older and perhaps more traditional notions and definitions of common sense is the shear capacity and universality of data's common sense role. Even if we talk of common sense as the 'basic human faculty that lets us make elemental judgements about everyday matters based on every day, real-world experience', or 'the truisms about which all sensible people agree without argument or even discussion', common sense remains a common property of humans in ways that data, even personal data, does not (Rosenfeld, 2011, p. 1). In the *datus quo*, with data as common sense, therefore, the only thing that matters is whether the data available are good or bad, and how to mitigate 'data credibility' problems to overcome or programme them out of systems, networks, and strategies (Redman, 2013).

Consent for the extraction and use of personal data remain vexed and contentious, suggesting that law has not yet found a reasonable balance between individual data subjects and those who view them only as sources for exploitation. As Peter Blume says, several important parts of data protection law presuppose 'the ability of the data subject to act as a data subject' (2015, p. 260). Not only must a data subject know their rights, but also law assumes them to give informed consent and assert those rights whilst acting at speed and with a voluntariness that describe most person's actions online (Blume, 2015, p. 260). Whilst data subjectivity is *prima facie* a legal status by definition, although precisely what this means this is something we will explore and question in more detail at different stages of this book, there is a more general, popular, or, perhaps we should call it post-legal assumption promoted by digital literacy and education that data subjects ought to know they are data subjects, and that they have, to echo Graham Harman's social theory of objects, reached or attained a new biographical stage called data subjectivity (Harman, 2018). These latter conceptualisations attempt to account, in the main, for individuals leaching personal data; individuals (data subjects) who either do not recognise or ignore, as fundamental to their online engagements and interactions, a *giving of themselves* that is constituent of personal data as a property of the individual (*proprius*).[3] It is important to note that the 'giving' I refer to here has little to do with the banal actions of sharing or exchanging personal information necessary to and promoted by social networks and platforms as habit-forming, user retention devices (Greenwald, 2014).

As a description that encompasses methods for creation and use of personal data and the effects on persons as data subjects, the *datus quo* has not remained fixed since becoming a feature of the Information Age in the latter half of the twentieth century. Yet, a combination of social, legal, and cultural principles underpinning definitions of data subjectivity have remained steadfastly narrow and unyielding to critique. As we shall see, law and regulations understand data subjectivity in terms of the individualism born of late twentieth century market capitalism and a person for whom privacy is a paramount concern as a self-proprietary, self-entrepreneurial matter. In a globalised landscape of personal 'datafication' and 'dataism' 'whereby life-processes must be converted into streams of data inputs for computer-based processing', privacy has taken on two complexions (Couldry and Yu, 2018, p. 4473). First, privacy defended or protected on behalf of the data subject (for example, paternal political models, but, equally, commercial and technological 'solutionist' models); second, privacy defended or protected by *sui generis* data subject as sovereign (for example, neo-liberal individual and entrepreneurial models). And between both models we find the role of transparency stipulated, for example, as 'a fundamental condition for enabling individuals to exercise control over their own data and to ensure effective protection of personal data', transparency as a gift of a protective regulatory regime but only where the data subject seizes the initiative and the advantages transparency affords to them.[4]

Personal data as a *giving of oneself* that can be superficial, profound, or perhaps nothing at all, is, therefore, an important departure from existing and narrow conceptions of data subjectivity. For example, when a range of commercial and non-commercial interests hungry for a valuable piece of each user online target and manipulate individual and group online behaviours and emotions, giving of oneself acts as a pause button.[5] This is because personal data are not only units or registers of a person's characteristics in the world on- or offline, such as a location pin in a map or a consumer preference log online ('cookies'). Personal data, as the prefix 'personal' constantly reminds us, is something ultimately offered, given, granted, or surrendered by fleshy and messy human persons to whom the data relates. As later chapters will discuss, both data subjects and the personal data to whom they relate are, arguably, 'objects' which ought to be considered more than their pieces and less than their effects (Harman, 2018, p. 53). We might say, for example, that as objects data subjects are assemblages or compounds of personal data objects, and are, therefore, more than their pieces. Equally, we might say that the pieces, each of which in this case is a personal data object, need not relate to a person at all; it only needs to relate to another personal data object. Both accounts presumably and radically transform normative definitions of the data subject by discrediting the data subject as the one to whom personal data relates. This is because each object, the data subject and the personal data, holds its forces in reserve and has an essence that escapes the grasp of legal, political and economic knowledge, understanding, and which definitions and framings cannot capture (Harman, 2016, p. 7).

The *datus quo* ultimately reflects, conceals, highlights, and marginalises varieties and conditions of personal data to fit the needs and desires of competitive market capitalism as the dominant socio-economic force. Humanity and global human endeavours are, almost without exception, shaped by free-market logics and neoliberal interpretations of capitalist economic reason that promote privatisation (as the withdrawal of state governance and intervention in favour of commercial and corporate governance), private property, and individualism. In the United States and United Kingdom alike, individual endeavour, often considered a striving against the odds ('bootstrapping'), linked to rights to property and privacy, have long been influential on law and policymakers.[6] Today governance bodies whether in public chambers or private boardrooms rely and draw extensively on computer analyses (scientific knowledge), modelling, and algorithmic parsing of free-flowing personal data (transborder data flows (TDFs)) to design policy initiatives, facilitate business growth, manage financial risk, and drive advertising revenue, or revenue from what Jaron Lanier calls 'behaviour modification feedback loops' (2019, p. 15). This stage in economic history will pass or more likely its own technologies will surpass or consume it.[7] Either way, personal data will outlive contemporary market logics as it predated them and the *datus quo* will shift. Personal data is not intrinsically a product of market logics, although its manipulation in and by competitive market forces makes it appear to be the case. As human imagination and intellect transcends markets and sees alternatives in the name of generosity and not greed, so too does personal data. Markets need personal data, but not *vice versa*.

Between ancient conceptions of *datus* and present characterisations of personal data is, perhaps, only the fact that data controllers and other stakeholders expect personal data today to harbour and deliver economic advantages, value, and reward (revenue, profit, etc.) at each stage of its giving and givenness. In whatever composition of metaphysical and empirical forms personal data have taken throughout history – Epicurus' association of the characteristics of atoms with the soul, for example – it has engendered value, but has not always had a price so inextricably linked to the profit motive (2012, pp. 98–105). 'Personal data is seen as a new asset', argues Sarah Spiekermann *et al.* referring to the World Economic Forum's description of personal data as a new asset class, 'because of its potential for creating added value for companies and consumers, and for its ability to enable services hardly imaginable without it' (2015, p. 161). Today the production, collection, processing, and leveraging of personal data happen with the aid of a constant slew of new surveillant and 'disruptive' technologies, networks, and systems designed and built to ensure maximum economic advantages from personal data by luring, titillating, and capturing the data subject as a source. Bernard Stiegler refers to the technologies that make this possible as 'technical supports of collective retention', the foundations of a new epoch of libidinal economy, which, when adjusted to social systems (or social networks), 'tend always to be forgotten, just as water is forgotten by the fish' (2019, pp. 13–14).

Acclimatised to online existence imbued with third-party and self-surveillance, data subjects have ceased to recognise personal data as a giving of oneself – as fish, they no longer see the water – and engage, instead, in rapacious online exchanges and consumption, all the while leaching personal data to those observing and waiting to collect. The inherent fishiness of datafication practices, including those associated with specific technologies, has led to the aquatic craniate theme appearing in several references to surveillance in trans-Atlantic discussions and debates (and repetitions) regarding personal data since the 1960s. The US Congressman for New Jersey, Cornelius Gallagher, who led a subcommittee into privacy and computers in 1966 referred to society moving into 'the blinding light of the Age of Aquarius which will become the Age of Aquariums, in which every action and every record is a fishbowl' (1970, p. 7). 'In the long run, but in the not-too-distant future', argued Leslie Huckfield, the Labour Member for Nuneaton, in the debate on the second reading of his Control of Personal Information Bill in 1972, 'society in this country will be what I can only call a goldfish society. We shall end up like goldfish swimming around in a bowl, every individual activity being observed and recorded' (Hansard HC Deb. vol. 835 col. 984, 21 April 1972).[8] In a supportive response to that Bill (in which he played a conceiving role), the legal academic Joe Jacob affirmed Huckfield's view whilst also echoing Gallagher, stating that 'this Bill recognizes the philosophical problems thrown up by the advent of the "Age of Aquariums" and has proposed an answer which is not exaggerated and which would be workable. It challenges', argued Jacob, 'the self-contained wisdom of technology and the self-confessed benevolence of the British bureaucracy', and where 'issues of liberty and the maintenance and progression of social norms are at stake', he concludes, 'neither of these should be taken on trust' (1972, p. 552). I view the consequences of this datafication fishiness as directly relating to individual control or a lack thereof, as expressed in the following statements that, despite being made several decades apart, describe two sides of the same coin. First, 'If they [data subjects] learned about today's volume and business done with their data among third parties', claim Spiekermann *et al.*, 'they may be surprised and feel betrayed' (2015, p. 165). Second, 'once it is felt that everything is being taken out of people's hands so that they have no control over their own lives', claimed Selwyn Gummer, the Conservative Member of Parliament for Lewisham speaking in the 1972 debate on the Control of Information Bill, 'it is difficult to call upon them to be responsible and reasonable human beings' (Hansard HC Deb. vol. 835 col. 990, 21 April 1972).

The capture, retention, and exploitation of an individual through the medium of their personal data is yet another way in which we expose the power relations that make up the global computational and info-economic fabric. For the data subject, like many subjectivities before them, as Marx and Engels maintained, 'all that is solid melts into air' (1992, p. 6). With a lack of understanding and certainty, the data subject is the person 'concerned at the growing amount of information they feel they have to give to "somebody up there", "they", "those in authority", the people who have power' (Hansard HC Deb. vol. 835 col. 1003, 21 April 1972). 'Both the individual and the population are beings beyond human perception', argues Evelyn Ruppert, 'and thus database devices are required to mediate and make them visible' (2012, p. 126). Confronted by the seemingly unstoppable, leaching of one's personal data into the world, and an attendant lack of clarity, certainty or security as to one's online status, nothing appears controllable. For data subjects all is in flux and uneasy – what I have referred to elsewhere as a state of 'data dysphoria' (Herian, 2020). Like fish suddenly aware of the water, perhaps also the bowl, the reaction is less a measured taking-back of control than a hypersensitive and panicked clawing-back or retreat – as in the withdrawal from social media accounts, albeit at the mercy of a stipulated deletion period upheld by the platforms in the hope the individual will change their mind and stay. Lack of control may only be a second-hand sensate or emotional response in the wake of other diverse effects driven by life lived online, but it is a powerful psychic need that inevitably forces its way to the foreground as part of a growing psychology of data ownership akin to the ownership of tangible assets and a reaction to obvious forms of exploitation (Spiekermann *et al.*, 2015, p. 165).

Data bank societies

Since the 1960s data subjects have rapidly developed into units of economic measure, a reserve army of (data) labourers, and embodiments of civic statistical value. Intertwining the three yet weighting, increasingly, towards the former two, commercial and private interests in many jurisdictions continue to consume spaces of public service and utility. Against this backdrop is a notable paradox in legal approaches to both personal data and the data subject, linked to commercial and civic interests, and involving the two caught between systemic fiscal demands (the need for 'digitally literate' data subjects to expose themselves to the impersonal, white heat of markets to drive economic growth and promote investment), and a countervailing protectionism rooted in individual self-sovereignty and rights to privacy. As a result, legislative constructions of personal data use and abuse (perhaps more accurately defined as abuse of privacy) have led to data subjectivity defined by the *necessity of its protection* in the likes of the EUs GDPR.[9]

The data subject has reached this present (yet still unsettled) legal status by the exercise of a peculiar set of cultural, political, economic, and social tensions perpetuated by the closing of boundaries-of-the-self using commercially available mechanisms of access and control and self-sovereignty to manage personal data, and a parallel opening-up through subservience and alignment to the authority of data markets and commodity conceptions shaped by neoliberal capitalism. Focusing on how commercial and non-commercial interests maintain the personal data and data subjectivity *status quo*, the aim of this chapter is to establish a baseline for the theoretical approaches in later chapters that will confront and challenge that *status quo*. To do so involves understanding personal data organisational and governance patterns in the last sixty years of the Information Age. We begin, therefore, in a post-war era amid public fears and expectations of so-called data bank societies in the United Kingdom, United States, and Europe.[10]

The aftermath of World War II unleashed organisational and bureaucratic theories and practices encompassing economic, political, and legal thinking, which shared in common the need for massive systems of data and information processing and retrieval. But data processing nor the use of relatively sophisticated machines to perform tabulation and calculation tasks were new. Punch card machines and, in particular, the Herman Hollerith data-processing system had been in use since the late nineteenth century. The appetite for personal data and its use in surveilling and shaping societies through data collection and the outsourcing of data processing by individual businesses and government was not a post-war phenomenon, but it assumed a new and far more ravenous character in the latter half of the twentieth century (Beniger, 1986, pp. 390–425; Yost, 2017, pp. 45–62). The American and Russian census' at the end of the nineteenth century were major testing grounds for Hollerith's system, and it was perhaps foreseeable that a suspicious public in those countries would view the process as an intrusion by their governments into private and domestic domains. Census data has long held an important place in statistical civic design methodologies and being an opportunity to confound or subvert those aims.[11] Discrete laws protect a national census, such as the *Census Act* in the United Kingdom, to gather 'statistical information with a view to ascertaining the social or civil condition of the population' (1920 c.41, Schedule s.1(6)). This does not mean that census data is sacrosanct nor subject to commercial exploitation.[12]

Long viewed with suspicion by individuals and communities much like those in the United States and Russia in the nineteenth century and perhaps rightly so, census collection shows early how data banks could and would emerge as prominent and influential tools for collecting and storing sensitive, personal information. The present discussion will not labour over material connections between census and other forms of data collection. The aim here is not to discuss the history of the census in the United Kingdom or elsewhere. But I raise the topic, albeit briefly, to show how easily translated technologies that improved the scale and efficiency of census counting were into other arenas of public and private life, including commercial sectors. As Meg Leta Ambrose has discussed in depth regarding the concomitant 'probabilistic revolution' heralded by 'the avalanche of numbers' in the nineteenth century, data collection was not only seen as means to greater efficiency but also to greater scientific knowledge and, thus, greater certainty that could be achieved in many fields, including law (2015). Hence, once the scale of time and cost efficiency savings of Hollerith's census counting became widely apparent, inevitably, a greater reliance on data ensued. There was no way for governments and, perhaps more importantly, businesses to unsee the power of data in decision-making and policy-forming. Nor, by extension, was it possible to roll-back the strategic and economic value of the technologies that collected and counted the data. As the American lawyer Thurman W. Arnold stated in his 1937 critique of laissez-faire capitalism in the United States, 'because machinery does in the long run promote higher standards, it is assumed that anyone pointing out a present problem caused by technological improvements is making an attack on the permanent utility of such improvements' (2000, p. 97). Technologies for the collection and storage of data, and the data itself, and the strategic use of both to help the 'bottom-line' were a clear sign of progress and a sure sign of a willingness to innovate.

The late nineteenth century and first half of the twentieth century, especially in America, Russia, and Germany, saw a parallel growth in bureaucratic ideas and electromechanical data processing and control in public and private sectors alike (Beniger, 1986, p. 422). World War II, as James Beniger suggests, stimulated information processing systems and advanced the great leap forward in computer technology that had started in the 1930s (1986, p. 406). Informatics systems and the technologies and operators that organised and controlled them assumed greater authority in global markets in the years following the war as investors and stakeholders sought angels from which to view and leverage efficiencies in private and public sectors and rationalise and speed up their own bureaucratic and regulatory processes.

In Western Europe, Japan, and the United States, an intensification of computer dependency occurred in industrial, commercial, corporate, and civic (i.e. state bureaucratic) settings in the wake of more sophisticated machines that included, for example, a shift from serial access memory, such as magnetic tapes, to random access memory (Beniger, 1986, p. 411).

In America between the World Wars, data-orientated bureaucracy provided by the likes of International Business Machines (IBM), underpinned and supported a wide range of business, government, and military needs. For example, coupled with automation in manufacturing, in the US data helped streamline processes, whilst the military used a rudimentary yet fundamental form of personal data, the individual measurements of recruits and enlistees (personal measurements *and* measurements of the personal), stored on individual punch cards to control the manufacture and distribution of uniforms (Beniger, 1986, pp. 420–421). For James Beniger, data processing pointed towards increased bureaucratic authority across society and, importantly, the development of new hardware (and eventually software) allowed such bureaucracies to grow and thrive by continuously controlling 'material processing and flows' (1986, p. 422). As glorified filing systems, early data banks, built around the bureaucratic tendencies unleashed by the likes of Hollerith, were a key feature of the new techno-social age which flourished from the middle of the twentieth century onwards. Data banks alone showed little spectacular from the point of view of the public. The atomic age forced its way into the global public imagination with the sublime image of the mushroom cloud. In parallel but stark contrast, the birth of the Information Age had no such symbols. Data banks and the bureaucracies they supported were by comparison opaque and boring, the original black boxes: forms of complex engineering whose internal workings were both hidden and understood by a relative few, to which we might add, uninteresting to the majority. Yet, data banks have proven equally if not more influential and transformational to society than atomic power through an increasing awareness of them in the public imagination of reflections of the very nature of society itself. As the first stanza of Felicia Lamport's poem, Deprivacy suggests:

> Although we feel unknown, ignored
> As unrecorded blanks,
> Take heart! Our vital selves are stored
> In giant data banks (Miller, 1971)

The burgeoning global Information Age that followed the war was a product of the endeavours and tools developed by science, engineering, and mathematics (many in the war, including the pioneering code-breaking and cryptography work of Alan Turing at Bletchley Park). But shifts in cultural perceptions of the computer and the data banks they connected to also play an important role. From basic calculating tools to 'beautiful machines' at the heart of total bureaucratic infrastructures capable of 'stitching' organising, storing, and manipulating data, information, people, and behaviour, computers and rapidly accessible data banks redefined economics and politics, and dragged the Information Age out of the laboratory and into wider society and the popular imagination (Hansard HC Deb. vol. 794 col. 867, 23 January 1970). Computers, data, and information were capable, it seemed, of reorganising humanity in such profound ways that comparisons could reasonably be made with forms of enculturation that created the first societies. As Beniger, writing thirty-five years ago but describing social patterns that remain prevalent today, maintains:

> Only since World War II have the industrial economies of the United States, Canada, Western Europe, and Japan appeared to give way to information societies, so named because the bulk of their labor force engages in informational activities and the wealth thus generated comes increasingly from informational goods and services. Although all human societies have depended on hunting and gathering, agriculture, or the processing of matter and energy to sustain themselves, such material processing, it would seem, has begun to be eclipsed in relative importance by the processing of information (1986, p. 426).

Within the post-war cultural shift that data processing and technologies caused, however, suspicions, fears, and uncertainty loomed large. For some, technologies were not *de facto* neutral or ineffectual, especially when accompanied by sinister ideologies or used by brutal regimes. As Brian Walden, the UK Member of Parliament for Birmingham, maintained in his speech on the Right to Privacy Bill in 1970: 'Modern technology has conferred substantial benefits on us. Moreover, it is foolish to regard bits of machinery as though they were human beings and had moral judgements and, therefore, could be labelled good or bad. Nevertheless, we cannot turn away from the fact that modern technology can be and is misused' (Hansard HC Deb. vol. 794 col. 863, 23 January 1970). Similarly, Leslie Huckfield in the debate on the second reading of his Control of Personal Information

Bill in 1972, claimed, 'we are now approaching the stage – indeed, we may already have reached it – where there are so many people in Government Departments and private companies and agencies gathering so much personal information on us all that our personal liberty, our personal privacy and our personal freedoms are already very much endangered' (Hansard HC Deb. vol. 835 col. 968, 21 April 1972).

In the artistic imagination, the coming social changes that computers and technologies heralded were more often than not dystopia in scope. The need to avoid the techno-moral nightmares alluded to by the likes of H. G. Wells, Yevgeny Zamyatin, George Orwell, and Aldous Huxley was an urgent mission variously cited by politicians and commentators alike amid a mixture of genuine attempts at action and copious amounts of handwringing. And yet, so often the attitude seemed to be one of capitulation to the inescapable path of human technological endeavours which made an Orwellian world, in particular, inevitable. Leslie Huckfield, in the same 1972 debate, mentioned a moment ago, highlighted the threat to personal integrity from the collection of mass information in computer profiles that 'will be even more real than the individual', admitting that he recognised the 'overtones of Big Brother and 1984', but that 'unfortunately it is a real risk in the near future' (Hansard HC Deb. vol. 835 col. 976, 21 April 1972). 'Mention computer, communication grids and data banks' quipped *The Times* newspaper in 1967, 'and it is easy to induce a mild hysteria in some people. The computer, an inanimate piece of machinery, is suddenly gifted with human powers and the threat of invasion of privacy is raised. The computer is to enslave us all, reduce us to mere ciphers, 1984 has arrived and big brother computer is watching us all' (Bonnett, 1967, p. viii). Writing at the same time, the American lawyer Arthur R. Miller was less jovial or dismissive of Orwell's (or Huxley's) fiction becoming reality:

As recently as a decade ago we could smugly treat Huxley's *Brave New World* and Orwell's *1984* as exaggerated science fiction having no relevance to us or to life in this country. But widespread public disclosures during the past few years about the new breed of information practices have stripped away this comforting but self-delusive mantle. It is now common knowledge that whenever a citizen files a tax return, applies for life insurance or a credit card, seeks government benefits, or interviews for a job, a new dossier is opened on him and informational profile is sketched. Indeed, there are precious few things left in life that will not leave distinctive electronic tracks in the memory of a computer – tracks that can tell a great deal about our activities, habits, and associations (1971, p. 39).

French sociologist Jacques Ellul writing in 1954 was equally keen to show that promises of technological progress also meant humanity's need to confront the possibility of divergent worlds. For Ellul, investment of human 'technique' in machines of technical productivity was nothing less than a means of explaining the restoration of man with the supernatural world 'from which he had been severed' (1964, p. 192). This was a severing that R. H. Tawney had also described a quarter of a century earlier, when he spoke of 'the fact that, unless industry is to be paralysed by recurrent revolts on the part of outraged human nature, it must satisfy criteria which are not purely economic' (1990, p. 278). The supernatural re-found by man through technologies such as the computer was, in Ellul's mind, 'a world full of promises that he knows can be realized and of which he is potentially the master' (1964, p. 192). Equally, however, it was a world Ellul saw beset with delirium, projected by man into a paradisal myth 'through which he can control, explain, direct, and justify his actions...and his new slavery' (1964, p. 192). 'The myth of destruction and the myth of action have', Ellul concluded, 'their roots in this encounter of man with the promise of technique, and in his wonder and admiration' (1964, p. 192).

Writing in 1956, the American sociologist C. Wright Mills observed in a more pragmatic tone:

> Most of the thirty-odd billion dollar corporations of today began in the nineteenth century. Their growth was made possible not only by machine technology but by the now primitive office instruments of typewriters, calculators, telephones, and rapid printing, and, of course, the transportation grid. Now the technique of electronic communication and control of information is becoming such that further centralization is entirely possible. Closed-circuit television and the electronic calculator put control of an enormous array of production units – no matter how decentralized such technical units may be – under the control of the man in the front office. The intricately specialized apparatus of the corporation will inevitably be more easily held together and controlled.
>
> (Mills, 2000, p. 123)

Less focused on the ephemerality of technique than Ellul and more on its stark and brutal contribution to US economic thrust, technology for Mill maintained a supernatural quality seen in its apparent omniscience and in the god-like control of 'the man in the front office'. 'There is a tale, apocryphal like most computer stories' that Malcolm Warner and Michael Stone tell in their 1970 critique of the data bank society that also picks up on the theme of computational godliness, 'of the biggest and latest computer, subjected to the full ceremonial of an official 'opening' by the President of USA'; they continue:

> Formalities, speeches, and switch-manipulation duly accomplished, the honoured guest was invited by the reception committee to submit a problem to the machine. With justified deliberation, unbecoming temerity, and commendable profundity, he fed in the question: 'Is there a God?' With scarcely a blink in its unwavering aplomb, with instanteous [*sic*] reaction, and abysmal theology, the computer replied: 'There is NOW' (1970, p. 17).

By the mid-1960s Herman Kahn and Anthony J. Weiner, in their 'speculation' on the world in the year 2000, maintained that: 'The capacity of the computer ultimately to effect a dramatic extension of man's power over his environment, as well as many other social and economic changes, is by now obvious to all' (1967, p. 87). While Warner and Stone saw the impact of computing on society as raising a spectrum of threats and promises, not least in how to approach the possibility of 'rule by computocracy' (1970, p. 15). On data specifically, Arthur R. Miller described information technologies giving birth 'to a new social virus – "data-mania"'(1971, p. 22). 'Institutions of almost every description are relying on the computer to increase their data-handling capacity and to improve the efficiency of their operations', declared Miller,

> The result is an inexorable pattern of establishing new data banks and converting existing information centers into ever larger and more complex computerized systems. As if spread with a magic nutrient, information systems of every size, shape, and form have sprouted and grown like weeds in recent years. As they do, their managers demand greater resources, more data on file subjects, and increased consolidation of separately maintained records (1971, p. 22).

Meanwhile, in the UK Parliament, members debating the Industrial Information Bill in 1968 were attempting to understand and describe the nature of technological change through the materiality of data and information, and the materiality of the means for storing and retrieving it. For example, the (aptly named) Labour MP and Minister of State, Board of Trade, Edmund Dell, spoke of how 'information is, in one sense, easier to come by, but, in another sense, it can often be more difficult to use when obtained' (Hansard HC Deb. vol. 775 col. 819, 13 December 1968). While Sir Edward Boyle, the Conservative

Party member for Birmingham, Handsworth who ushered in the second reading of the Bill, described the shift in public understanding of information because of technology in the following material terms:

> Within a few years from now industrial information may no longer be thought of primarily in terms of written imprints in a book or blueprint drawings, but rather as holes on cards, magnetic fields on tapes and discs, electrical impulses moving through the memory core of a computer, or even radiations generated in vats of complex chemicals. Furthermore, when computer systems are interconnected by some modern communications vehicles, like television, satellites and laser beams, we will have the capacity to move larger quantities of information over vast distances in units of time so imperceptible that they are difficult to comprehend.
>
> (Hansard HC Deb. vol. 775 cols. 803–804, 13 December 1968)

As a function of the state, the military and national defence played (and continue to play) significant roles as 'domains', to use W. Brian Arthur's terminology, in which technological innovations developed and subsequently became embedded in civilian society (2010, pp. 73–74). Echoing Ellul's notion of the extension of military 'technique', notable developments in civilian societies included tools and methods of surveillance and long-range communications (1964, p. 229). In the United States in the decade immediately following World War II, as C. Wright Mills highlights, 'Scientific and technological development, once seated in the economy, has increasingly become part of the military order, which is now the largest single supporter and director of scientific research in fact, as large, dollar-wise, as all other American research put together' (2000, p. 216).

We can find several domains and techniques between private and public interests. In the last sixty years governments and commercial interests, often with military partners, have shaped characterisations of personal data and the benefits and purposes of personal data or what this ought to be. Surpassed or superseded by the value of information and its raw form, data, knowledge value has, in many senses, diminished. As the Liberal Member of Parliament for Orpington, Eric Lubbock outlined in his speech during the Right to Privacy Bill debate in 1970 quoting John Hargreaves, a board member of IBM:

> how greatly the situation changes when the means of technology and communication allow the entire dossier of an individual to be held on a small segment of magnetic tape, and how much greater

the temptation to use it. The trail of records as he passes from cradle to grave can be accumulated relentlessly. He starts life as a birth certificate and quickly becomes a tax allowance. He generates education records: his personality and IQ can be categorised and his programmed instruction can be geared to his needs. He enters the world and becomes a working, housing, medical, social, service, and perhaps criminal statistic. He accumulates licences for dogs, television, cars and marriage. He leaves behind him, as he moves through life, records of purchases and debts, mortgages and earnings, successes and failures, travel and change, interests, hobbies, clubs, activities, friends and associates. It is not too much to see the possibility of this process starting before birth with a determination of his genes, and to presume that, as he eventually leaves this world, he is merely 'Passed for further consideration and comment.

(Hansard HC Deb. vol. 794 col. 932, 23 January 1970)

For much of the post-war period the sources of personal data (consumers, citizens, etc.) have not been party to decisions made about how the collection or use of personal data by government or commercial interests nor offered the opportunity to influence personal data exploitation or if, how, where, or when personal data enters systems and networks of value. Warner and Stone identified this as contributing to an ethical problem involving failing to criticise pervasive computer usage and errors at the hands of computers 'attendant acolytes' (1970, p. 14). For Ellul, the matter was squarely one of economics and not an issue with the machines used for its improvement. 'Whereas the overpowering phenomenon of the machine strikes home to everyone and makes plain its influence on economic life', argued Ellul, 'the ways of economic technique are secret and everyone remains convinced of its innocuousness and docility' (1964, p. 159). And yet, it seems, there was a clear logic introduced by technology in post-war bureaucracies that impregnated economics (law, politics, and wider social and cultural life as well), one which had been in play since Hollerith introduced his system to the world at the end of the nineteenth century. A logic that involved complex vectors reduced to reasonably straightforward steps – identified by Warner and Stone as 'more information, more rational judgements. Better data, better decisions. More facts, more power' — which some people did (and do) call progress, while others regard it as techno-social and techno-moral tyranny (1970, p. 20). Either way, at the centre of this mass data proliferation was and is a data subject, weathering the storm and risking harm in the face of powerful information flows.

Assault on the data subject

We might legitimately argue that the 'pursuit of big data has created an army of cyber vampire squids, relentlessly jamming their blood funnels into anything that smells like it could be monetized' (O'Shea, 2019, p. 17). Personal data scandals, such as the ones involving Cambridge Analytica and Facebook in the wake of the 2016 UK European Union Referendum and US Presidential election, appear marginally capable of shaking people from a stupor by causing moral outrage. Scandals do prompt questions, if not always or precisely transformations in or criticisms of the febrile relationship between personal data, commercial interests, and governments which underpins daily existence for billions of people worldwide (Wong, 2019). Amid the Covid-19 pandemic it is already clear that personal data is playing and will continue to play a decisive role in tracking the virus. This means levels of surveillance of personal data across populations never seen before or imagined, both in terms of the monitoring of individual and group location and movement, 'external surveillance', and biometrics (e.g. body temperature), behaviour patterns or even emotion and mood, 'internal surveillance'. People have become familiar with the former and even welcomed it in recent decades, notably when it offers benefits for geospatial mapping applications such as Google Maps, the latter, however, is far more contentious, even though here we have also seen, for example, widely adopted body monitoring and tracking devices aimed at improving health, well-being, and athletic performance such as Fitbit.

Whether external or internal, however, the certainty of escalation in personal data monitoring will inevitably mean the further and potentially more profound erosion of privacy which may be a step too far for some and yet another scandalous assault on the data subject for others. Should it take a scandal to achieve this level of outrage or prompt these questions? As we have seen, Malcolm Warner and Michael Stone believed it necessary to criticise and question the rationale of computer use and application at every turn in order for a society to function in harmony with its technologies. Whilst the vastness of computer control today challenges the feasibility of Warner and Stone's principle, it remains a salient and vital one. Testing whether something as definitive or visceral as an 'assault' on the data subject occurs is important because of the legal and regulatory ramifications this state of affairs engenders. But it is also important because it highlights fine lines between awareness and ignorance of the consequences of lives lived online.

The proprietary relationship of a subject to 'their' or 'my' data is exceedingly nuanced (Rees, 2013, p. 221). It is easy to claim that Facebook breached the trust between the corporation (platform) and its subscribers (users) when it allowed Cambridge Analytica to harvest personal data from approximately 50 million profiles (Cadwalladr and Graham-Harrison, 2018). Or that the breach was a product of both shameless exploitation and the ignorance of Facebook users as to the value of the data. This description is unsatisfactory, however, because many users are not ignorant of the part personal data plays in social networks and similar platforms as both a retention device (users sharing and swapping information about themselves with 'friends'for instance), a product, or the basis of highly lucrative advertising revenue, which keeps platforms 'free' (Spiekermann *et al.*, 2015, p. 161). As a Communication from the European Commission on approaches to personal data protection published in 2010 stipulated, 'technology allows individuals to share information about their behaviour and preferences easily and make it publicly and globally available on an unprecedented scale' (p. 2). Nick Srnicek points out that, 'data extraction is becoming the key method of building a monopolistic platform and of siphoning off revenue from advertisers' (2017, p. 58). Further, that users are, in fact, regularly exploited by social networks and platforms in ways plain to see but which do not seem to offend or discourage a majority who, anyway, rarely, if ever, read or digest verbose end-user agreements that would alert them to the declared legal status of their data.[13] 'The compulsion that alienates humans and tries to compel them to use capitalist Internet platforms is social in nature', argues Christian Fuchs (2016, p. 102). He continues: 'Capitalist Internet companies threaten to alienate human beings from their own social nature by giving them the feeling that they will miss out on social opportunities and by the circumstance that they may be treated as outsiders if they do not use specific platforms' (Fuchs, 2016, p. 102). If use of the network and services Facebook provides means giving up something of oneself in the process to take part and be a relentless target for advertisers, so be it. Data subjectivity is not, on this account, something many users ('natural persons' rather than 'legal persons', a distinction fundamental to present data protection laws in Europe and the United States) relate to as they casually scroll through newsfeeds, liking posts, leaving comments, posting pictures and links, and leaching personal data.

Apart from the moral outrage driven by, what may more accurately be the mis-exploitation of personal data in cases such as the one involving Cambridge Analytica and Facebook, uncertainty regarding privacy is arguably the first, real legal consideration for most individuals. Evidence of a breach of privacy is equally the first taste of what it means to be a data subject rather than a mere user of a network, platform, or service. Focusing on the problem of privacy and the encroaching uncertainties of technologies and the 'global village' in the late 1960s and early 1970s, Arthur R. Miller's work examined American's socio-legal position and concluded that so much personal data and information, once considered private, 'is now considered to be appropriate grist for the computer mill and fair game for the data collector' (1971, p. 23). For Miller, the erosion of individual privacy at the hands of technologies and those who promoted them as the very definition of assault in the Information Age. Similarly, Warner and Stone recognised that the prospect of the 'global village' was 'as likely to promote tyranny (or more broadly, oligarchy), as it is to encourage universal Rousseauite hippydom' (1970, p. 27).

Dominant platforms today, namely Facebook, Google, Netflix, Amazon, and Uber that Nick Couldry and Ulises Mejias collectively refer to as the 'social quantification sector', show the accuracy of Warner and Stone's predictions of oligarchy (2019). Some commentators see these platforms as far worse than their robber baron predecessors because they pose 'fearsome threat whose ambitions to control our future politics, media, and commerce seem without limits' (Kotkin, 2017). The materiality of Miller's 'grist to the mill' metaphor reminds us that personal data is both a vital essence and a lucrative asset. Commercial actors may not appreciate the vitality of personal data, but they absolutely recognise it as lucrative and adjust business models and strategies ad infinitum to extract every drop of value from stores of personal data. Speaking in the parliamentary debate that followed publication of the Younger Committee Report into privacy in 1973, Shirley Williams, the Labour Member of Parliament for Hitchin, stressed:

> It is true that private data banks and, one is bound to say, Government data banks in certain respects have sold information for commercial purposes – for example to provide address lists for purposes other than that for which the information was originally obtained. A considerable question therefore arises [...] It is the question of what sort of access there is to data, what controls there are for its use for a purpose other than that which it was obtained.
> (Hansard HC Deb. vol. 859 col. 1978–1979, 13 July 1973)

Writing nearly half a century later, Rob Lucas highlights an ongoing and similar concern in his review of Shoshana Zuboff's *The Age of Surveillance Capitalism*:

> Businesses were concerned only with 'transaction value', viewing the end consumer merely as a means. Combative relationships with

consumers were the symptoms of a 'transaction crisis'. If businesses could only make a Copernican turn to the end consumer, they would find a world of pent-up 'relationship value'. They would need to draw on new technologies, saving costs through merging digital infrastructures and orientating to the provision of 'support' configured to the individual. The projected economic 'revolution' seemed to involve the generalization of something like the executive's personal assistant (2020, p. 132).

Political and commercial debates, narratives and discourse from the latter half of the twentieth century, especially those which directly influenced policy and legislative development, reveal some generational shifts in the commercial embodiment of and assault on the data subject. Equally, they show that some things have been slow to change, if they have changed at all. For example, echoing Shirley Williams speaking in 1973, a Competition and Markets Authority (CMA) report in the United Kingdom highlighted that, 'Firms have always sought information on actual and potential customers but the advent of digital, connected technologies have allowed this to happen on a much greater scale, with greater range and more quickly than ever before' (2015). It is maybe trite to say that an already vast scope of data collection is increasing exponentially, as massive data storage solutions both improve in terms of compression and grow in terms of physical infrastructure.[14] But we do well to remind ourselves of this, to recognise what is at stake from mass datafication, because, as Spiekermann *et al.* claim, 'due to Internet users' apparent comfort with sharing their data, more and more organizations today engage in the trading of consumer data, operating in legal grey zones when it comes to handling personal information assets' (2015, p. 162).

Post-industrial intellectual institutions, information platforms, and markets heavily reliant on personal data are far from transparent about where data comes from or how it is used to generate value. Against this backdrop the latter half of the twentieth century has seen an upward shift in baseline computer know-how, competences, and, broadly, a higher degree of online self-awareness among consumers and citizenry alike concerning the 'value' of personal data. As a result, Stuart Biegel highlights, by the millennium 'a turning point was reached' in the backlash against indiscriminate gathering of personal information, and he pinpoints disclosure by the large Internet advertising firm DoubleClick that they had created a program that matched consumer identities with anonymous data that had been gathered (2001, p. 68). As already suggested, however, educating consumers into technology literacy, adoption, and use does not mean personal data exploitation decreases. It broadens the range and availability of sources to work with. The invention of the smart phone as a single, convenient point of commercial and governmental contact and access to billions of data subjects has undoubtedly made easier this easier. Since 2007 smart phones have sped up and enlarged the scale of cyberspace and manifestly, increased the computational power an average person wields daily. This has allowed data subjects to flourish. With a smart phone data subjects can do and be more, in the truest sense of capitalist labour principles, a data subject can be more productive. In 2018 alone, estimations of global sales of smart phones to end users were 1.56 billion.[15] Therefore, the amount of personal data produced and disseminated both knowingly and unintentionally by smart phone users, by data subjects, also manifestly increased and continues to increase (Spiekermann *et al.*, 2015, p. 161).

Technological solutions to the anxieties resulting from a loss of control over personal data privacy and identity seem ubiquitous today. But the realisation that such solutions might be or are warranted because of a rapid growth in the capacity and speed of computer systems and networks threatening individual personality is not recent, nor, it seems, the preserve of ideological or party-political bias in British political history. It was, for example, highlighted by the Labour Member of Parliament for Stoke Newington and Hackney North, David Weitzman, quoting in his speech during the debate following publication of the Younger Committee Report, a line from that Report which stated that 'privacy is a basic need, essential to the development and maintenance both of a free society and of a mature and stable individual personality' (Hansard HC Deb. vol. 859 col. 1987, 13 July 1973). And in the same debate, Richard Hornby, Conservative Member of Parliament for Tonbridge similarly stated that, 'the concept of privacy is a fundamental concept to man in society, and particularly to man in a highly industrialised, technological and crowded society such as ours' (Hansard HC Deb. vol. 859 col. 1992, 13 July 1973). Finally, the Labour Member for Nuneaton, Leslie Huckfield who offered a critique of the findings of the Younger Report. 'My concern', Huckfield declared, 'centres around the need of the individual, despite the fact that we live in a well-organised community, occasionally to opt out of it to an extent to which I believe he has some right to govern. I am concerned about the right of the individual to obtain some kind of anonymity and above all the right, to a certain extent at any rate, to be left alone' (Hansard HC Deb. vol. 859 col. 2023, 13 July 1973).

Under the sway of new and emergent technologies and encryption it is easy for the individual to feel a sense of self-control and self-sovereignty over personal data and believe that the power to control identity and personal data rests in personal devices, and, conversely, that the assault on the data subject is less tenable or in decline. The problem is the assault has not gone away, only changed form. To further echo Leslie Huckfield's criticism of the Younger Report, to believe the assault has gone away is a 'failure to recognise that information today is power. It is the failure to recognise that the gathering of information is the acquisition of power' (Hansard HC Deb. vol. 859 col. 2023, 13 July 1973). Where once commercial practices including the exhortation of advertisers and marketeers were a reasonably direct and blunt tool which were constrained by a relatively narrow spectrum of advertising channels, now it is often intrinsic to and tailormade for the online experience of the data subject. Promotion, marketing, and advertising are all woven into the fabric of social networks and can be indistinguishable from ordinary commentary or 'news', appearing as friendly recommendations by bots or algorithms that encourage us to look at products and content. The commercial exhortation to look and buy does retain a human form though with influencers and creatives paid by corporations and brands, large and small, to act as cybernetic billboards and 'global marketing solutions' embedded in or acting as the focal point of discrete online communities.[16]

The assault on the data subject has not ceased, therefore, only taken on friendly and more inviting external forms, and decidedly more sinister and problematic internal ones such as an autoimmune-like response that turns the assault inwards on the data subject whilst continuing to drive more and greater production and leaching of personal data into the world. Moreover, a certainty vanity arises in the data subject who is pressed constantly to protect 'their' data and 'their' privacy from intruders marking them out as a special case for attention. This is clearly not the case. Masses of personal data do, for better or worse, create a lumpen data subjectivity in which 'my' data is no more or less valuable, distinguished, or important than anyone else's. As John Page, the Conservative Member of Parliament for Harrow, pithily retorted in the Control of Personal Information Bill debate in 1972: 'let us have a genuine control of all access and let us have a code of conduct, but let us not pretend that every vital statistic about ourselves is a vital as all that' (Hansard HC Deb. vol. 835 col. 999, 21 April 1972). But what is law's response to the assault on data subjects? What protections can the law offer and how do these interact with economic interests and markets in free-flowing personal data?

Notes

1. GDPR Article 4 – Definitions
   (1) 'personal data' means any information relating to an identified or identifiable natural person ('data subject'); an identifiable natural person is one who can be identified, directly or indirectly, in particular by reference to an identifier such as a name, an identification number, location data, an online identifier or to one or more factors specific to the physical, physiological, genetic, mental, economic, cultural, or social identity of that natural person

   Data Protection Act 2018 (incorporating GDPR)

   3 Terms relating to the processing of personal data
   (1) This section defines some terms used in this Act.
   (2) 'Personal data' means any information relating to an identified or identifiable living individual (subject to subsection (14)(c)).
   (3) 'Identifiable living individual' means a living individual who can be identified, directly or indirectly, in particular by reference to –
      (a) an identifier such as a name, an identification number, location data or an online identifier, or
      (b) one or more factors specific to the physical, physiological, genetic, mental, economic, cultural, or social identity of the individual.
   (4) 'Processing', in relation to information, means an operation or set of operations which is performed on information, or on sets of information, such as—
      (a) collection, recording, organisation, structuring or storage,
      (b) adaptation or alteration,
      (c) retrieval, consultation or use,
      (d) disclosure by transmission, dissemination or otherwise making available,
      (e) alignment or combination, or
      (f) restriction, erasure or destruction, (subject to subsection (14)(c) and sections 5(7), 29(2) and 82(3), which make provision about references to processing in the different Parts of this Act).
   (5) 'Data subject' means the identified or identifiable living individual to whom personal data relates.
2. http://archives.nd.edu/cgi-bin/wordz.pl?keyword=datus (accessed 31 March 2020).
3. Later chapters will explore the notion of personal data as property in the legal meaning of the term that supports an extensive rights regime designed to facilitate *inter alia* ownership, possession, protection, and access to property. Here, however, I use the term in a broader sense of a material, constituent part or characteristic of something larger – *proprius* meaning, at once, own, individual, special, and characteristic (http://archives.nd.edu/cgi-bin/wordz.pl?keyword=proprius (accessed 31 March 2020)). In this case, bits and bytes (1 byte = 8 bits) of personal data from a larger body of personal data as well as a larger intellectual and fleshly body of an individual to whom those data relate.
4. Communication From The Commission To The European Parliament, The Council, The Economic And Social Committee And The Committee Of The Regions (a comprehensive approach on personal data protection in the European Union) COM/2010/0609 final, p. 6.

5. This sort of behavioural and emotional manipulation, conducted by unwitting and unaware participants, is well documented in a mass experiment conducted on 689,000 Facebook users for one week in January 2012, which concluded that 'emotions expressed by other Facebook influence out own emotions, constituting experimental evidence for massive-scale contagion via social networks' (Kramer *et al.*, 2014, p. 8788).

6. For example, in a debate on privacy in the UK Parliament in 1973, the Secretary of State for the Home Department at that time, Robert Carr, stated: '[privacy] is something which at different times we all need and its presence or absence is a useful measure of the quality of life in our society. A society which attaches importance to privacy is almost by definition a society which also attaches importance to the individual generally' (Hansard HC Deb. vol. 859 col. 1956, 13 July 1973).

7. As I write the world is dealing with the Covid-19 pandemic, as the later chapter will discuss in more depth, which has emphasised certain technologies and a desire to expand their range of use, such as artificial intelligence (AI) to track the movement of the virus through populations, and blockchains to increase the resilience of international supply chains. In the United Kingdom, media reports demonstrate concern for the health and mental well-being of the nation in lockstep with concerns for the national and global economy. The pandemic has revealed inherent and often extreme vulnerabilities in the global economic system. Markets, unable to countenance the present global uncertainty, are rising and falling arbitrarily and in ways which seem even more detached from reality than usual. Right-wing governments around the world are turning to measures including the nationalisation of industries implying free-market competitive capitalism might suit the good times but socialism works. Although, as 'national socialism' there is now real concern of the actualisation of fascism in right-wing led countries struggling to maintain democratic orderliness.

8. Even though it was published a couple of years after, Foucault's reading of Bentham's panopticon is clearly echoed in Huckfield's 'goldfish bowl' analogy. Although Huckfield's interest in control of personal information turns on a belief in the need to educate and inform the public about information and data use and misuse, rather than an express fear that it will be used to discipline and punish individuals, there is an unmistakable alignment between Foucault and Huckfield on encroaching threats of surveillance and the power of surveillance not only to monitor but equally to shape behaviour.

9. Regulation (EU) 2016/679 of the European Parliament and of the Council of 27 April 2016 on the protection of natural persons with regard to the processing of personal data and on the free movement of such data, and repealing Directive 95/46/EC (General Data Protection Regulation).

10. The reference draws on the book of the same name, see Warner and Stone (1970).

11. The so-called Jedi census phenomenon is a contemporary example involving large numbers of people in the UK and Australia listing their religion as Jedi, the fictious knights in the Star Wars films. See, for example, Ahmed (2016).

12. See, for example, https://www.ons.gov.uk/census/2011census/2011cen susbenefits/howothersusecensusdata/businessandcommerce (accessed 18 April 2020).
13. A well-rehearsed illustration of this in law and technology scholarship concerns so-called 'click-wrap licenses', basic contracts and end-user agreements relating to software and application that we all, invariably, click agreement to without bothering to read the detail. As Yochai Benkler points out:

> the vast majority of users are unlikely to pay close attention to license details they consider to be boilerplate. This means there is likely significant information shortfall on the part of consumers as to the content of the licenses, and the sensitivity of demand to overreaching contract terms is likely low. This is not because consumers are stupid of slothful, but because the probability that either they would be able to negotiate out from under a standard provision, or a court would enforce against them a truly abusive provision is too low to justify investing in reading and arguing about contracts for all but their largest purchases. (2006, p. 446).

14. Data storage capacity is predicted to reach 470 exabytes by 2021. https:// www.statista.com/statistics/638593/worldwide-data-center-storage-capacity-cloud-vs-traditional/ (accessed 19 April 2020); see also, the Amazon Web Services sponsored whitepaper, Mohan and DuBois (2016).
15. https://www.statista.com/statistics/263437/global-smartphone-sales-to-end-users-since-2007/ (accessed 16 March 2020).
16. See, for example, https://influencer.com/ (accessed 20 April 2020).

References

Competition and Markets Authority. 2015. *The Commercial Use of Consumer Data: Report on the CMA's Call for Information*. https://assets.publishing. service.gov.uk/government/uploads/system/uploads/attachment_data/file/ 435817/The_commercial_use_of_consumer_data.pdf (accessed 18 March 2020).

European Commission. 2010. *Communication from the Commission to the European Parliament, The Council, The Economic and Social Committee and the Committee of the Regions COM(2010) 609 Final*. https://eur-lex.europa.eu/ LexUriServ/LexUriServ.do?uri=COM:2010:0609:FIN:EN:PDF (accessed 25 July 2020).

United States Congress. 1970. *Mailing Lists: Hearings, Ninety-first Congress, Second Session, on H.R. 2730 and Similar Bills. July 22 and 23, 1970*. US Government Printing Office.

Ahmed, Tufayel. 2016. 'Star Wars' Fans Urged Not To List Religion as Jedi on Australia Census Form. *Newsweek*, 8 May. https://www.newsweek.com/ star-wars-fans-australia-dont-put-jedi-your-census-form-487647 (accessed 18 April 2020).

Ambrose, Meg Leta. 2015. Lessons from the Avalanche of Numbers: Big Data in Historical Perspective. *I/S: A Journal of Law and Policy for the Information Society*. Vol. 11, No. 2, pp. 201–277.

Arnold, Thurman W. 2000. *The Folklore of Capitalism*. Washington, DC: Beard Books.

Arthur, W. Brian. 2010. *The Nature of Technology: What It Is and How It Evolves.* London: Penguin.

Beniger, James R. 1986. *The Control Revolution: Technological and Economic Origins of the Information Society.* Cambridge: Harvard University Press.

Benkler, Yochai. 2006. *The Wealth of Networks: How Social Production Transforms Markets and Freedom.* New Haven: Yale University Press.

Biegel, Stuart. 2001. *Beyond Our Control? Confronting the Limits of Our Legal System in the Age of Cyberspace.* Cambridge: The MIT Press.

Blume, Peter. 2015. The Data Subject. *European Data Protection Law Review.* Vol. 1, No. 4, pp. 258–264.

Bonnett, J. H. 1967. Guarding the Secrets. *The Times*, September 15.

Cadwalladr, Carole and Emma Graham-Harrison. 2018. Revealed: 50 Million Facebook Profile Harvested for Cambridge Analytica in Major Data Breach. *The Guardian*, 17 March. https://www.theguardian.com/news/2018/mar/17/cambridge-analytica-facebook-influence-us-election (accessed 19 April 2020).

Couldry, Nick and Jun Yu. 2018. Deconstructing Datafication's Brave New World. *New Media & Society.* Vol. 20, No. 12, pp. 4473–4491.

Couldry, Nick and Ulises A. Mejias. 2019. *The Costs of Connection: How Data Is Colonizing Human Life and Appropriating It for Capitalism.* Stanford: Stanford University Press.

Ellul, Jacques. 1964. *The Technological Society.* Translated by John Wilkinson. New York: Vintage.

Epicurus. 2012. *The Art of Happiness.* Translated by George K. Strodach. London: Penguin Classics.

Floridi, Luciano. 2013. *The Ethics of Information.* Oxford: Oxford University Press.

Fuchs, Christian. 2016. *Reading Marx in the Information Age.* Abingdon: Routledge.

Greenwald, Ted. 2014. Under the Influence. *Wired*, 16 October. https://www.wired.co.uk/article/under-the-influence (accessed 19 April 2020).

Harman, Graham. 2016. *Immaterialism: Objects and Social Theory.* Cambridge: Polity.

Harman, Graham. 2018. *Object-Orientated Ontology: A New Theory of Everything.* London: Penguin.

Heidegger, Martin. 2011. *Basic Writings.* Edited by David Farrell Krell. Abingdon: Routledge.

Herian, Robert. 2020. Blockchain, GDPR, and Fantasies of Data Sovereignty. *Law, Innovation and Technology.* Vol. 12, No. 1, pp. 156–174.

Jacob, Joe. 1972. Computers and Privacy – a British Answer. *Anglo-American Law Review.* Vol. 1, No. 4, pp. 544–552.

Kahn, Herman and Anthony J. Weiner. 1967. *The Year 2000: A Framework for Speculation on the Next Thirty-Three Years.* New York: The Macmillan Company.

Kotkin, Joel. 2017. Today's Tech Oligarchs Are Worse Than the Robber Barons. *The Daily Beast*, 13 April. https://www.thedailybeast.com/todays-tech-oligarchs-are-worse-than-the-robber-barons (accessed 24 March 2020).

Kramer, Adam D. I., Jamie E. Guillory and Jeffrey T. Hancock. 2014. Experimental Evidence of Massive-Scale Emotional Contagion Through Social Networks. *Proceedings of the National Academy of Sciences of the United States of America*. Vol. 111, No. 4 (June 17), pp. 8788–8790.

Lanier, Jaron and Jim Euchner. 2019. What Has Gone Wrong With the Internet, and How We Can Fix It: An Interview With Jaron Lanier. *Research-Technology Management*, May–June, pp. 13–20.

Lucas, Rob. 2020. The Surveillance Business. *New Left Review*, Jan/Feb, pp. 132–141.

Marx, Karl and Friedrich Engels. 1992. *The Communist Manifesto*. Edited by David McLellan. Oxford: Oxford University Press.

Miller, Arthur R. 1971. *The Assault on Privacy: Computers, Data Banks, and Dossiers*. Ann Arbor: The University of Michigan Press.

Mills, C. Wright. 2000. *The Power Elite*. Oxford: Oxford University Press.

Mohan, Deepak and Laura DuBois. 2016. *Leveraging the Breadth of Storage Services and the Ecosystem at AWS – Unlock the Full Potential of Public Cloud IaaS*. https://d0.awsstatic.com/analyst-reports/US41693416.pdf (accessed 24 April 2020).

O'Shea, Lizzie. 2019. *Future Histories: What Ada Lovelace, Tom Paine, and the Paris Commune Can Teach Us About Digital Technology*. London: Verso.

Redman, Thomas C. 2013. Data's Credibility Problem. *Harvard Business Review*, December. https://hbr.org/2013/12/datas-credibility-problem (accessed 22 May 2020).

Rees, Christopher. 2013. Tomorrow's Privacy: Personal Information as Property. *International Data Privacy Law*. Vol. 3, No. 4, pp. 220–221.

Rosenfeld, Sophia. 2011. *Common Sense: A Political History*. Cambridge: Harvard University Press.

Ruppert, Evelyn. 2012. The Governmental Topologies of Database Devices. *Theory, Culture & Society*. Vol. 29, No. 4/5, pp. 116–136.

Spiekermann, Sarah, Alessandro Acquisti, Rainer Böhme and Kai-Lung Hui. 2015. The Challenges of Personal Data Markets and Privacy. *Electronic Markets*. Vol. 25, No. 2, pp. 161–167.

Srnicek, Nick. 2017. *Platform Capitalism*. Cambridge: Polity Press.

Stiegler, Bernard. 2019. *The Age of Disruption: Technology and Madness in Computational Capitalism*. Translated by Daniel Ross. Cambridge: Polity Press.

Tawney, R. H. 1990. *Religion and the Rise of Capitalism*. London: Penguin.

Warner, Malcom and Michael Stone. 1970. *The Data Bank Society: Organizations, Computers, and Social Freedom*. London: George Allen & Unwin Ltd.

Wong, Julia CarrieJulia Carrie. 2019. The Cambridge Analytica Scandal Changed the World – But It Didn't Change Facebook. *The Guardian*, 18 March. https://www.theguardian.com/technology/2019/mar/17/the-cambridge-analytica-scandal-changed-the-world-but-it-didnt-change-facebook (accessed 19 April 2020).

Yost, Jeffrey R. 2017. *Making IT Work: A History of the Computer Services Industry*. Cambridge: MIT Press.

2 Somewhere between privacy and protection

Introduction

Law has a problem keeping pace with the innvations and technologies that service and, increasingly, shape the needs of society. The Internet, World Wide Web, associated communication and information technologies and personal mobile devices, and the resultant growth in personal data that has ensued from the transnational (and transjurisdictional) mass adoption and feverous use of each have made law's task complex.[1] 'Global computer-based communications cut across territorial borders', as David Johnson and David Post remarked in an early treatise on cyber law in the Internet Age, 'creating a new realm of human activity and undermining the feasibility – and legitimacy – of applying laws based on geographic boundaries', concluding 'this new boundary defines a distinct Cyberspace that needs and can create new law and legal institutions of its own' (1996, p. 1367). Even if laws designed for an offline world can be just as effective online and in different technological or device-intensive contexts negating need for distinct cyber laws, revising or adjusting laws and regulations to address vexed issues posed in and by the multifaceted dimensions of cyberspace, and across attendant information and computer technologies, is no mean feat (Jones, 2018). As Christopher Rees suggests, 'we should not be surprised to find that for us, in the early years of the Information Age, there is a ferment as the law seeks to find appropriate ways of dealing with the new age's most significant asset and common currency: Information' (2013, p. 220).

The last chapter introduced the key issue of the assault on the data subject, a commercial and non-commercial aim to extract personal data to enact efficiency gains and drive revenue. I also suggested that the assault was as much self-inflicted by data subjects (autoimmunity), including by those acting as, what Byung-Chul Han calls, entrepreneurs of the self – individuals not as subjects but projects 'always refashioning and reinventing' themselves (2017, pp. 1–2). 'It is not so much that the information is dangerous to the individual or useful to the compiler but that both of these may be true', argued the legal academic Joe Jacob in a brief article, 'the possibility of the utility of the information', he continued, 'gives the impetus to create the data bank; the possibility that the information will be used for mischievous purposes creates alarm' (1971, p. 20). In his assessment of the final report from UK Government's Committee on Data Protection in 1979 (chaired by Sir Norman Lindop), James Durbin echoed Jacob's sentiments, claiming that the 'thought that personal information, perhaps incomplete or inaccurate, might be cheaply and easily available to others without control or regulation, and might be used to the detriment of an individual, possibly without his knowledge, is repugnant to most people' (1979, p. 300). In so far as it can command the *datus quo*, law's response to the assault on data subjects is of paramount concern. As the previous chapter showed, and Adam Warren and James Dearnley claim, data protection legislation in the United Kingdom and other European countries stemmed from a growing reliance on collecting personal data, 'and from the realization that unfettered collection and distribution of personal documentation and data potentially or actually placed individual privacy at risk' (2005, p. 239). What safeguards and protections can the law offer, and, importantly, how do these interact with economic interests, including those of entrepreneurs of the self, and markets in free-flowing personal data?

Delayed and haphazard regulatory and legislative interventions, constraints, and protections, including myriad legal and extra-legal doctrines and principles, all intertwine in contexts of information and communication technology, but rarely to the benefit of clarity. This has been the case for many decades in Western countries seeking policies to protect personal information, especially those, such as the United Kingdom and United States, that pride themselves on being liberal democracies that place great emphasis on the autonomy of the individual and the limitedness of the government (Regan, 1984, p. 19). In the United Kingdom the first serious debates and attempts by Parliament to legislate to meet a growing nexus of privacy concerns, computer use, and personal data collection did not begin until the late 1960s with the *Industrial Information* Bill, when data banks were already firmly entrenched in the bureaucratic and commercial infrastructure of the nation, if not yet in its unconscious or popular imagination (Hansard HC Deb. vol. 775, 13 December 1968). Privacy largely dominated parliamentary debates and activities, although often interwoven with distinct concerns for individual security as the means of preventing infringements of privacy (Tapper, 1977, p. 198; Warren and Dearnley, 2005, p. 245). Along with two key Committee reports, the Younger Report in 1973 which examined privacy and the Lindop Report in 1978 (mentioned above) which focused on data protection alongside privacy, and the exception of the *Consumer Credit Act* 1974 which allowed access to personal data albeit in specific circumstances, UK lawmakers began slowly climbing the rungs on a long ladder to direct legislation that would finally pass in the mid- and late 1980s, namely the *Data Protection Act* 1984 and *Access to Personal Files Act* 1987 (Regan, 1984; Warren and Dearnley, 2005).

Some observers saw early what was at stake from the rise of computing and the commercial desire for personal data and, in hindsight, with notable foresight. For example, in his failed attempt to pass legislation on a right to privacy in 1970, Brian Walden, the Labour Member of Parliament for Birmingham, made a statement in his parliamentary speech that reads like a prediction of today's social media fetish for posting, exchanging, and sharing personal information that inevitably leads users to cross-post information about others, imposing 'privacy externalities on each other' and eroding the freedom 'about which the British people care most', the right to be left alone (Hansard HC Deb. vol. 794 col. 862, 23 January 1970; Spiekermann *et al.,* 2015, p. 163). 'We have to endure the tedium of reading in print the pimples and problems of café society', Walden argued, 'and perhaps it is because of that that the feeling has grown up that, somehow, a longing for privacy is a remnant of a more savage existence, a vestigial remain of a feeling which sophisticated man should have got rid of, and that the really "with it" person should be prepared to expose his tastes and peccadilloes before the world for its entertainment and enlightenment' (Hansard HC Deb. vol. 794 col. 862, 23 January 1970). Set against a backdrop of rapacious business models hungry for personal data and burgeoning markets for personal data tied, increasingly, to global credit and finance, legal interpretations of personal data and the data subject have become ever more complex and unwieldy. Yet the law could not provide consistent or convincing frameworks to deal with the social and cultural changes wrought by technologies and the upsurge in primacy of personal data in particular. But, then again, is it too much to ask of the law in the first place?

The UK Parliament has spent decades debating various effects of computerisation in public and private domains and the proliferation of personal information and data. Yet still these matters, perhaps a sense of control and regulation of technologies, continue to evade the grasp of lawmakers. In the Right to Privacy Bill debate in 1970, several speeches acknowledged that the law was not capable of meeting the challenge of the Information Age. Sir John Foster, the Conservative Member of Parliament for Northwich for example, raised concerns over the 'computerisation of all available information', suitable remedies for people who lacked control over false information held about them deliberately or by mistake, and widespread abuses by electronic systems against which English law had very little to say (Hansard HC Deb. vol. 794 col. 907, 23 January 1970). In the 1972 Control of Information Bill debate, the Minister of State for the Home Office, Mark Carlisle, argued that 'what the computer has done is to bring to the fore the degree of the problem', which he considered being 'the safeguarding of information, the security of the files in which the information is contained, and the integrity of those who have the keys to the places where the information is stored', concluding that 'above all, the problem is the use of that information in a way which appears to people to interfere with that they believe are their rights to privacy' (Hansard HC Deb. vol. 835 col. 1006–1007, 21 April 1972).

Similarly, in the parliamentary debates that followed publication of the 1973 Younger Committee's Report into privacy, including the impact of computers and data banks on privacy, Shirley Williams, the Labour Member of Parliament for Hitchin, highlighted privacy concerns that had arisen because of a 'massive technological revolution which we in our wisdom have to try to use for good and not evil', one involving greater 'speed of access and capacity of storage of computers', 'great technical strides [...] in devices capable of watching, listening and tracing human beings', and 'increase surveillance techniques and the use of surveys as a method of gaining information' (Hansard HC Deb. vol. 859 col. 1974, 13 July 1973). Whilst subsequent parliaments have addressed to some extent the challenges set out by John Foster and Shirley Williams half a century ago and in the intervening years lawmakers in the United Kingdom and elsewhere have become familiar with technologies and the spirit of innovation that drives them, those challenges remain extant, even germane to the present moment. Law has found no solution for the challenges, instead they remain legal blind spots motivated, at least sometimes, by an interlinking of economic growth and desires to innovate without boundaries. As Roger Brownsword maintains: 'The consensus is that collection and use of personal data needs governance and that big data-sets (interrogated by state of the art algorithmic tools) need it a fortiori; but there is no agreement as to what might be the appropriate terms and conditions for the collection, processing and use of personal data or how to govern these matters' (2019, p. 329).

Complexity around personal data has induced a streamlining of consumer information on personal data at both national and supranational levels in recent years. Insights and distillations produced by the likes of the Information Commissioners Office (ICO) in the United Kingdom promote 'openness by public bodies and data privacy for individuals', whilst attempting to demystify data subjectivity.[2] Bodies such as the ICO are, arguably, more welcome than not, but offer a form of digital education and literacy for consumers in agreement with the incontestable value of consumer frameworks, and with information adhering to homogenised frameworks of personal data use, abuse, and alienation that only touch on notions or practices of exploitation concerning a special protection status, notably for children. But informing or educating persons as data subjects does not make knowing what data subjectivity ultimately means any easier to grasp. Like any subjectivity constructed by and because of impersonal systems and networks, the creation of data subjects occurs in the hybridisation or compounding of both online and offline social and cultural systems and networks. In the Information Age data subjectivity is as inevitable as it is inescapable, it is not a consumer choice.

Initial resistance to 'transborder data flow' (TDF) reflected concerns of sovereign nations that the development and use of TDF's will undermine 'informational sovereignty', impact on the privacy of local citizens, and upset private property interests in information (Johnson and Post, 1996, pp. 1371–1372). 'But efforts to control the flow of electronic information across physical borders – to map local regulation and physical boundaries onto Cyberspace', were, as Johnson and Post predicted, futile, especially in countries participating in global commerce (1996, p. 1372). The legal status (interests, rights, duties, and obligations) of data subjects, data controllers, and other personal data stakeholders acting within today's free-flowing global data marketplaces, has reached legislative and regulatory apexes with General Data Protection Regulation (GDPR) in Europe and, within the patchwork of federal and state data protection and privacy provisions in the United States, the California Consumer Privacy Act (CCPA), which came into force in January 2020. There is neither time nor space to rehearse data protection laws in the United Kingdom, Europe, the United States, or elsewhere at length. The previous chapter described the social and cultural backdrop from which many of these legal measures were born. But excavating the data subject from laws that do not account for it in rich and thorough ways requires looking at current and dominant legal positions and definitions, while also seeking to account for, as Spiekermann *et al.* usefully highlight, 'strategic data subjects who maximize the value of their personal data and therefore engage in strategic behaviour, such as avoiding leaving traces' (2015, p. 163). As I previously suggested, the *datus quo* describes a tension between data laws as we find them and arguments that those laws do not sufficiently capture, describe, or account for the data subject as a principal and heterogenous subjectivity.

Considering social effects caused by the Covid-19 pandemic, we can even now say with a much greater level of certainty that the data subject is the principal subjectivity in societies and communities lived simultaneously on- and offline. The curtailing of much sociality because of the pandemic means that online life is one of the few options remaining for social expression. Information and communication technologies have been closing the gap between virtual communities and offline realities for some time, but the global pandemic has sped up that process. This echoes what Brownsword refers to as 'the ubiquitous mediation of modern technologies in the accessing, acquisition, transmission, exchange, and processing of information, the breadth and depth of our reliance on these technologies and the extent to which all of this contributes to the generation of new information' (2019, p. 300). To better understand data subjectivity, or, perhaps, to recognise the ineffability of it that escapes conceptualisations and legal conceptualisations specifically leaving it ignored or unrecognised by the law, means appraising what we can already see.

The art of privacy

Almost without exception, data protection regulations and legislation the world over have at their core privacy considerations (Lucente and James Clark (eds.), 2020). Privacy in terms of data protection is heterogenous and encapsulate a variety of features including individual human rights, community values underpinned by strong privacy considerations, and temporal notions of erasure and forgetting (as in Article 17 of the GDPR known as the 'right to be forgotten'). Encouraging and offering guidance on the protection and security of personal data privacy is, in a majority of jurisdictions, overseen by a combination of data commissioners, authorities, and officers who broadly perform the same actions, including informing business and the public about rights and policies regarding data use and enforcing breaches of domestic codes (Spiekermann *et al.*, 2015, p. 161; Lucente and Clark (eds.), 2020). We might also see this process as bringing an individual to an understanding and identification of their rights and interests. And this may refer to access, exclusion, and control regarding property and privacy rights and interests intertwined in an individual sense of identity and personality, discussed both positively and negatively by lawyers and technologists alike (*eBay, Inc. v. Bidder's Edge, Inc.*, 100 F. Supp. 2d 1058 (N.D. Cal. 2000); Benkler, 2006; Rees, 2013, pp. 220–221; *Spiekermann et al.*, 2015, pp. 161–167; Posner and Weyl, 2018). Priscilla Rider claims that, 'as long as there are human beings in the world each one will have his problem of how to obtain his permitted benefits, and how to determine his personal obligations. The importance, then, to the individual, of preserving his total-identity is more than an abstract concept; it is a very real and practical necessity' (1959, p. 32). Whilst for Arthur Davidson, the Labour Member of Parliament for Accrington speaking in the debate on the Control of Personal Information Bill in 1972, the growing expectations on the individual to surrender information about themselves to public and private sector organisations alike underpinned a real threat of 'depersonalisation' (Hansard HC Deb. vol. 835 col. 1003–1004, 21 April 1972). The 'excessive use of computers depersonalises people', Davidson argued, 'they become unemployment statistics rather than unemployed persons. They are figures in an opinion poll rather than people who have expressed political views. I may become "a typical example" rather than me, and I would rather be me than a typical example' (Hansard HC Deb. vol. 835 col. 1004, 21 April 1972).

Legal reappraisals, if not entirely or always reforms or reinterpretations, of the links between personal information, data protections, and privacy rights and interests happen with each fresh wave of information and communication technology. But Rider's claim that privacy derives, in part, from the preservation of identity remains central to data subjectivity specifically and digitalised ontologies more generally. Interestingly, we can see not only the preservation of Davidson's depersonalisation at work in today's society – opinion polls continue to function as Davidson describes - but also the power of technology companies, brands, and manufacturers to convince billions of consumers that their personality is inextricability linked to the personal devices they own. These two points, Rider's and Davidson's, converge in the contemporary realm of sophisticated personal encryption devices which may yet prove a challenge for business models trading in personal data and needing to engage with and keep data subjects as sources but protected by a bundle of data privacy, identity, and property rights and interests.[3] To foster enterprises and markets in personal information and data, Spiekermann *et al.* argue, requires novel end user devices that 'empower individuals to manage their personal data', a practice that would 'establish a strong base for the user's digital identity', but this is open to debate and criticism (2015, p. 161; Käll, 2018; Manski and Manski, 2018; Herian, 2020). We will consider personal data as property further in later chapters.

Whilst privacy has been a central question for Western philosophy for millennia, legal interest in the subject and the formulation of jurisprudence on privacy is barely a century old. Aristotle's distinction between the administration, governance, and management of the state or political realm (*polilikos*) and of the household or domestic realm (*oikonomia*) (1992); John Locke's distinction between public and private rooted in property theory (2013); and Hannah Arendt's notion of privacy given meaning by its opposition to the public realm, one in which everything 'can be seen and heard by everybody and has the widest possible publicity', show the enduring and insoluble struggle for humanity to understand the nature of privacy (2000, p. 199). And yet jurisprudence committed to individual privacy rights – crystallised in the very concept of 'the right to privacy' – only emerged in the late nineteenth century, with many citing Samuel D. Warren and Louis D. Brandeis' Harvard Law Review article directly addressing the right to privacy, or lack thereof, as the catalyst.

In reaction to Warren and Brandeis' work, definitions of privacy have touched upon different characteristics often classed as fundamental to the human condition, with some showing consideration for tensions between privacy and technologies that, in some senses, continue Warren and Brandeis' legacy and speak to the present. For example: 'the individual's ability to control the circulation of information relating to him – a power that often is essential to maintaining social relationships and personal freedom' (Miller, 1971, p. 25); 'the right not to be interfered with when one is engaged on one's lawful occasions' (Hansard HC Deb. vol. 859 col. 1999, 13 July 1973); privacy as a cluster of rights that is 'not a distinct cluster of rights but itself intersects with the cluster of rights which the right of the person consists in and also with the cluster of rights which owning property consists in' (Thomson, 1975, p. 306); privacy as 'control over who can sense us' (Parker, 1974, pp. 280–281); 'the condition of not having undocumented personal knowledge about one possessed by others'

(Parent, 1983, p. 269); creation of a 'context in which both deceit and hypocrisy may flourish' (Schoeman, 1984, p. 199); 'a necessary condition for something of basic value – the development of an autonomous self' (Kupfer, 1987, p. 81); or 'a view of privacy as the norm that regulates and structures social life' (Becker, 2019, p. 307).

Nineteenth century privacy considerations linked to – it is important to note – technological changes in, amongst other things, press and personal photography, may well be the acorns from which have grown the royal oaks of contemporary data privacy. Relative to 'the advancing density of our social organisation', the contexts in which individuals exist and covert privacy today differ from the nineteenth century (Hansard HC Deb. vol. 794 col. 944, 23 January 1970). People have to navigate points between traditionally conceived or planned public and private spaces, and between hybridised, compounded, augmented, virtual, and often hyper transient domains. But, arguably, the basic grounds for privacy protection outlined by lawmakers have not changed despite the significant changes in context, however.[4] An individual's choice to forgo social media to preserve privacy is a contemporary practical example of this. As Priscilla Rider suggests, 'the obscure person has a more perfect right of privacy than the less obscure' and this echoes the choice to stay away from social media; and yet, pervasive use of social media by one's friends and family is no guarantee that privacy is absolute, hence even 'the obscure person may involuntarily lose the benefit of this right' (1959, p. 41).

Publication of an individual's personal details in ways that could offend or embarrass may once only have been possible or likely through the medium of newspapers, with certain information protected by laws of defamation and breach of confidence, and self-regulatory codes of good practice and ethics of decency upheld by the press. Today pervasive dissemination of personal information and misinformation, or the piecing together of disaggregated bits, nibbles, and bytes of personal data to similar ends, and the attendant risk of falling foul of laws of defamation is an opportunity widely available to anyone with requisite technical know-how or just a Facebook account and a grudge to bear (Spiekermann *et al.*, 2015, p. 163; *Voller v Nationwide News Pty Ltd; Voller v Fairfax Media Publications Pty Ltd; Voller v Australian News Channel Pty Ltd* [2019] NSWSC 766). 'The digital versions of most publications along with broadcasting channels, search engines, and social media services', Rees highlights, 'already serve to be the vehicles by which most 'news-worthy' information is provided to the public' (2013, p. 220). Explaining her theory of contextual integrity in online privacy, Helen Nissenbaum states that:

> The theory of contextual integrity offers [...] learned wisdom from mature systems of informational norms that have evolved to accommodate diverse legitimate interests as well as general moral and political principles and context-specific purposes and values. The promise of this path is not merely that equilibriums achieved in familiar contexts may provide analogical guidance from online realms; rather, the path acknowledges how online realms are inextricably linked with existing structures in social life. Online activity is deeply integrated into social life in general and is radically heterogenous in ways that reflect the heterogeneity of off-line experience (2011, p. 37).

Individual experience and a mass psychology of privacy on- and offline both have weighting in understanding contemporary data subjectivity and the phenomenon of being in personal data. The desire to be 'left alone', a pillar of Warren and Brandeis' right to privacy argument in the nineteenth century, even though not the only concern surrounding personal data today, remains central to the matter of the individual 'bits' and 'bytes' of personal data that make up the greater free-flowing mass of analysable data, ripe for processing into valuable information. As Lucian Floridi argues, 'The right to be left alone is the right to be allowed to experiment with one's own life, to start again, without having records that mummify one's personal identity forever, taking away from the individual the power to mould it' (2013, p. 246). Notwithstanding the underlying privilege in Floridi's outline of identity – does everyone really have the means (time, space, money) to experiment with their life as Floridi suggests? – a demand to be left alone is something of a childlike injunction shouted at a world of potential risk, harm, and impropriety. But it resonates with the Information Age as an age of immediacy, acceleration, and emotional response expressed in moments often without pause for consideration or rehearsal. 'We need privacy', argues Joseph Kupfer, 'to rehearse our thinking and behaviour, to try out options without running "real life" risks', something which applies to 'virtual, online life' equally (1987, p. 83). Self-promotion and sharing on social media platforms involve tensions between data subject exposure and withdrawal, exploitation and consent – to be or not to be left alone – that are vital to understanding the emergent nature of data subjectivity in the twenty-first century.

Data subjectivity involves freneticism, confusion, anxiety, and unconscious desires to be retained (liked, needed) by the networks and systems that one uses, or to which one subscribes, and into which one leaches personal data, constantly and effortlessly, into the world. Law's primary task ought to ensure limits to the exploitation of the data subject are in place (but able to expand), remain difficult to breach, or that no incentive to breach is obvious or attractive to data controllers and stakeholders. Incentives, therefore, play an important role. 'These days there is far too much material available on all of us', argued Brian Walden in a section of his speech in the 1970 Right to Privacy Bill debate that touched on incentives relative to privacy and data banks, whereas in the past, he continued,

> we at least had the consolation, for what it was worth, of knowing that that information was lying around all over the place, and that the problem of getting it together was likely to be prohibitive in terms of economic cost and would involve a great deal of labour on the part of the person who wanted to collect it. That was some reassurance, but that has now gone. The computer [...] is ideally suited doing what, in the past, I have said it was unable to do, namely, to stitch together all the information that can be found out about us from any source, starting with school records and going right through every aspect of our private lives if it should be in somebody's interest to do so, and it will be. Let us have no doubt about that.
>
> (Hansard HC Deb. vol. 794 col. 866–867, 23 January 1970)

Taking for granted that Brian Walden was correct in his estimation of how computers would challenge privacy and undermine prior incentives based on the onerous manual labour of gathering information 'by hand', not only offering incentives but also promoting codes of good practice, clear principles, both political and ethical, which run deeper than legal procedural and doctrinal norms is one answer to law's fundamental inability to keep pace with technological innovation. In the same debate as Brian Walden, Alexander Lyon, Labour Member of Parliament for York, raised a similar concern. 'It is the principle of how far the freedom to protect your private life ought to interfere with the freedom of someone else to find out about your private life', stated Lyon, 'it is the principles rather than the methods of intrusion which are of the essence of this problem, and the principles can ben decide only in comprehensive legislation' (Hansard HC Deb. vol. 794 col. 889, 23 January 1970).

Whether legislation, codes, principles, or ethics can prove effective in the fluidity and flux of the Information Age is an open question, however. For Manuel Castells any reasonable ethical foundation is questionable given 'the "spirit of informationalism" as a culture of "creative destruction" accelerated to the speed of the opto-electronic circuits that process its signals. Schumpeter meets Weber in the cyberspace of the network enterprise' within a mode of capitalism where 'the corporate ethos of accumulation, the renewed appeal of consumerism, are driving cultural forms in the organization of informationalism' (2010, pp. 214–215). Discussing the approach of technology companies such as Google to ethical concerns operating within an 'Enlightenment-era pro-information bias', Evgeny Morozov maintains that, 'questions of ethics – of whether it's right or wrong to organize information and increase its usefulness – are never posed. Instead, Google is preoccupied solely with questions of efficiency, for it presumes – and given our Enlightenment bias, rightly so – that few could challenge its ends' (2014, p. 86). In identifying patterns in the approach of lawmakers to privacy and data protection, several key legal instruments since World War II are instructive, but raise questions of whether appropriate safeguards have been fulfilled and whether they can meet what Joe Jacob referred to as, 'misplaced desires for efficiency', and what spirit – economic, political, cultural, legal – those safeguards ultimately represent or satisfy (1971, p. 20).

What Morozov describes is, for Byung-Chul Han, the second Enlightenment, an 'age of purely *data-driven* knowledge', which prompts the need for a third Enlightenment 'to shine a light on how digital enlightenment has transformed into a new kind of servitude' (2017, p. 58). Han's Hegelian position is apparent and to some extent defensible, although it may be far too optimistic. In his post-enlightenment ideal, Han appears to concede that the anarchic individualism of cyberspace – the sort celebrated by John Perry Barlow (1996) – must give way to an age in which the (newly) enlightened individual realises herself in proportion to the extent of her surrender to something larger than herself.[5] The problem is what should assume the place of something larger than the individual in this context, and who gets to decide? As I have discussed elsewhere, new technologies such as blockchains and associated applications including tokens and cryptoassets like Bitcoin problematise the ideal still further (Herian, 2018). Whilst absorption into the mainstream has nullified some radical elements of Bitcoin it was undeniably a new outgrowth of anarchic individualism in cyberspace, or, with some concessions to Han (and Hegel), at least a new outgrowth of discrete anarchic and individualistic communities to which individuals could surrender. The point is, if a new digital enlightenment were possible along the lines Han describes, it would likely be anti-digital and seek to encourage a retreat from all forms of digitalisation to escape the servitude that comes with it. I do not disagree that there is a problem of servitude in cyberspace and relating to the use of information and communication technologies. Personal data extraction, exploitation, and forms of 'prosumption', whereby consumers online produce surplus-value for platforms who pay them no wage, are types of servitude enacted by corporate and government power (Fuchs, 2016, p. 97). Dismissing technologies or even retreating from cyberspace are no longer realistic propositions. Barring the catastrophic collapse of global social organisation and infrastructure, we need to live better with technologies and the benefits they ought to afford everyone.

Appropriate safeguards

In 1948 the Universal Declaration of Human Rights – 'a standard by which to judge competing philosophical theories about human rights' and, therefore, the *'enlightened* conscious of mankind' [emphasis added] (Morsink, 1984, p. 309) – established a marker for the future of privacy rights, putting the world on notice of a shift in the rights, duties, and obligations of the individual in society. The 12th fundamental right guarantees that: 'No one shall be subjected to arbitrary interference with his privacy, family, home or correspondence, nor to attacks upon his honour and reputation. Everyone has the right to the protection of the law against such interference or attacks'.[6] Two years later, nations in the community that would become the European Union (EU) signed a comparably 'enlightened' declaration, with Article 8 of that declaration guaranteeing everyone, 'the right to respect for his private and family life, his home and his correspondence'; but also introducing key derogations 'in the interests of national security, public safety or the economic well-being of the country, for the prevention of disorder or crime, for the protection of health or morals, or for the protection of the rights and freedoms of others'. An individual's right to privacy in Europe, in an echo of longstanding principles in law, was not absolute but qualified to protect economic efficacy and discourage social disorder. Privacy was, therefore, defined not so much as an individual right but a socially structured privilege permissible in the fair weather of international and domestic peacetime and a robust economy.

It would take two more decades before the mission set-out in the Universal Declaration would meet expansive new realities of mass data gathering, storage, use, and exchange processes. The Freedom of Information Act (FOIA), brought into force in the United States in 1967, channelled the Universal Declaration of which the United States had been not only an enthusiastic signatory, but also opted for Europe-style derogations. Given the FOIA incorporated the elements of the Universal Declaration but tempered them with significant caveats linked to the darkest recesses of government secrecy, this immediately put in doubt the 'freedom' in the title of the Act. In his privately signed statement for the FOIA instead, perhaps ironically, of the usual public signing of Bills, President Lyndon B. Johnson described the vital place information held in American society and the need to protect individual rights and freedoms, but highlighted that the greater good ('the welfare of the nation'), including defending national security, 'may require that some documents not be made available'.[7]

The tension between the absoluteness of the Universal Declaration and qualified positions driven by national interests in both the European Declaration and FOIA portrays situations in which governments rallied around legitimate concerns. The Cold War was in full flight at the time President Johnson signed the FOIA into law and national security, much as it does today, easily trumped individual interests in the mind of a government fearful of enemy surveillance and intelligence capabilities. But, whilst national security measures are relatively straightforward limitations on the expression of individual privacy rights to gauge, economic arguments, such as protecting national economic well-being, are less clear-cut and show mere economic determinism as a political decision. It would be absurd to anthropomorphise economy and the upticks, depressions and inequalities every economy undergoes as being equivalent to human emotional highs and lows. Economy or specific features of it, such as inequality, are perhaps best understood, as Thomas Piketty suggests, as deeply political and the 'joint product of all relevant actors combined' and not reducible to 'purely economic mechanisms' (2014, p. 20).

Despite the early interventions in data and information processing legislation and apparent gestures of goodwill to its citizenry, Europe overtook the United States in the 1970s onwards in its urgency to develop a legislative framework that could meet the needs of an ever-closer union of technology and economy. Germany was at the forefront of Europe's resurgent authority in datafication practices, with the world's first data protection legislation adopted in 1970 in Hessen, followed in 1974 by Rhineland-Palatinate, and in 1977 by the Federal Data Protection Act (Freude and Freude, 2016). Following on the heels of the Council of Europe's convention on data protection in 1981, the United Kingdom finally reached a milestone in domestic legislation with the *Data Protection Act* 1984, after parliamentary debates spanning three decades and the final two-tone realisation of the public's 'lingering unease' concerning computers and data banks, and that 'thanks to computers the use, transmission and communication of information is becoming daily both more complex and more proficient' (Hansard HC Deb. vol. 40 col. 553–554, 11 April 1983). Following the politico-economic approach highlighted by Piketty which is also the prevailing and dominant narrative regarding informational technology innovation in both the United Kingdom and EU, William Whitelaw, Secretary of State for the Home Department at the time of the Data Protection Bill debates in 1983, maintained that:

> The great majority of computer systems are, as they say in the trade, "subject friendly" – that is, they benefit those about whom information is stored. If we are to continue to improve efficiency and productivity, maintain our trading competitiveness, and keep up the service that Governments supply to the citizen, we must ensure that the information technology industry flourishes. The [Data Protection] Bill provides the individual for the first time with a general right of access to data held about him and it requires the registration of the holding and use of data. Together with the guidelines on privacy protection of the OECD, the convention offers an international standard for data protection. This has provided us with a yardstick against which to measure our own proposals. Our intention is to ratify the Council of Europe convention, and we have kept its provisions firmly in mind in drafting the Bill. The Bill takes from the convention eight general principles which are set out in schedule 1 – principles which owe their origins to the work of the Younger committee in this country more than a decade ago. The principles relate to the use which is made of data – the way in which data are collected, held and disseminated. They require data to be used only in accordance with the purpose specified for them and they provide for the quality of the data in question – accuracy, relevance and so on. The principles establish a right of access for data subjects to the data held about them, and provide for the correction or erasure of the data where appropriate. They require adequate security measures to be taken to protect the data.
>
> (Hansard HC Deb. vol. 40 col. 553–555, 11 April 1983)

Notable about the Data Protection Bill debates was the key role of privacy in protecting computer or automated processing of personal data. Privacy and data protection, despite attempts to separate the two conceptually in terms, for example, of a difference between the value of information and sensitivity of the information, remained stubbornly conjoined (Tapper, 1977, p. 200). Roy Hattersley, speaking for the opposition Labour Party in the same debate and as 'that most lowly of all persons, the data subject, one of the 50 million people for whom the Bill ought to provide protection' maintained that the government had not gone far enough in instilling the privacy protections necessary (Hansard HC Deb. vol. 40 col. 560–561, 11 April 1983). Hattersley maintained that 'a Data Protection Bill essentially should be part of a general policy to preserve and protect the right of the individual to keep his affairs private and secret if he or she wishes to do so. The protection of data is only one part of the concept of the right to privacy. Until the majority of the House is prepared to give its support to that general principle, the privacy that we seek will not be obtained. It will not be obtained by a measure as limited as this' (Hansard HC Deb. vol. 40 col. 561, 11 April 1983). Once it became law, the 1984 Act proved weak on privacy. This was, in part, because the Act did not 'regard legal persons as data subjects' (Willis, 1994, p. 70). 'Given the general legal background in the UK, which does not recognise a general right of privacy, and the fact that the primary motivating factors for the adoption of the DPA [Data Protection Act] in 1984 seemed to have been economic not philanthropic', argued Sarah Willis, 'the DPAs apparent balance against privacy is arguably not surprising' (1994, p. 70).

The marriage of individual privacy rights and protections with economics now embedded in GDPR fosters exposure of the date subject to markets and encourages a fusing of legal, economic, and data subjectivities as the same and in ways that breach the limits on the opportunism of private companies and public agencies that Roy Hattersley had in mind (Hansard HC Deb. vol. 40 col. 561, 11 April 1983). As a result, under the aegis of a right to data protection and self-determination over personal data that flows directly from the inalienable rights of the individual, the average European citizen carries a daily burden of potentially conflicting statuses: as a free market, free-flowing data subject, and a private, shielded, rights-bearing data subject (Freude and Freude, 2016). For Peter Blume this ought not to be the case, although he recognises that consent may be a burden for the data subject rather than a safeguard (2015, p. 261). 'Data protection law has additional purposes related to the digital economy and e-government', maintains Blume, 'but the main reason for its existence is the consideration of the data subject and the recognition that they need dedicated legal protection in the digital age' (2015, p. 258). Far from solving the intractable problem of adjusting free-flowing data to data protectionism, Europe embraced a contradictory position and continues to move forward under GDPR with a data regime constantly in search of compromise and harmony.[8]

In a critical commentary on Directive 95/46/EC before GDPR, Roger Brownsword and Morag Goodwin implore future EU legislation to disentangle the data protection regime, lest it be 'pulled in different directions', creating a tension that 'no amount of clever drafting can overcome' (2012, p. 310). 'Although the 1995 regime hints at the difference between informational privacy and data protection pure and simple', argue Brownsword and Goodwin, 'it leaves too much to interpreters' (2012, p. 310). Adopting a regulatory viewpoint that both echoes the limitations of the FOIA and affirms the strengths of the Universal Declaration, they continue:

> If the free circulation of data is to be restricted only for general reasons of fairness, openness and acceptability, there will facilitative ground rules for online processing of personal data without individuals having a strong veto of the kind of represented by the privacy right. Such facilitative ground rules might find some space for the expression of personal preferences; but they will not be comparable to the power of a right-holder to prevent the circulation of data by declining to give consent to access it in the first place or to its onward transmission. So long as the focus is on the facilitation of the circulation of data, the regulatory controls (for the protection of the interests of data subjects) will primarily be procedural; in other words, the collection and circulation of data will need to be done in the right way. However, where the focus is on respect for the fundamental right of privacy, regulators will largely leave it to the individual to determine whether data can be accessed and circulated. In the one case, individuals who transact or interact online will do so on terms that regulators judge serve the public interest (striking an appropriate balance between the free flow of information and transparency); individuals, thus, will have little control over their personal data, by contrast, in the other case, the regulatory protection of privacy rights puts individuals in a key controlling position. So long as the tension is unresolved, while those whose priority is free circulation of data will see the regulatory restrictions as obstructive (particularly if there are

heightened restrictions of the kind that one would expect where privacy rights are engaged), those whose priority is the protection of privacy rights will see the regulation as confused and ineffective.
(Brownsword and Goodwin, 2012, p. 310)

Despite continuing adherence in most jurisdictions to privacy principles established by the Universal Declaration, privacy and data protection definitions across jurisdictions, in common and civil law jurisdictions alike, differ and are inconsistent. For the EU, the 1995 Data Protection Directive was a 'milestone in the history of the protection of personal data' and enshrined 'two of the oldest and equally important ambitions of the European integration process: the protection of fundamental rights and freedoms of individuals and in particular the fundamental right to data protection, on the one hand, and the achievement of the internal market – the free flow of personal data in this case – on the other' (European Commission, 2010, p. 2). But around privacy and protection also circulate other legal and quasi-legal concerns, such as confidentiality, fairness, transparency, and consent, and it is on these factors that further issues of regulatory consistency and divergence across jurisdictions occur. 'Most often, a set of data protection principles that inform privacy laws include rights and obligations such as data minimization, legitimate use, purpose binding, and informed consent', claim Spiekermann *et al.*, but these 'principles leave little room for market negotiations between the data subject and the data controller, let alone between third parties', resulting in some firms using 'enforcement gaps or regulatory arbitrage between jurisdictions to engage in the trade of personal data' (2015, p. 162). It is implicit in the principles of the GDPR, for example, that it protects individuals from discriminatory consequences derived from the processing of their personal data, and Article 5 states that personal data must be processed 'fairly'. Further, GDPR maintains that data processing based on consent must be freely given for it to be valid, and it does not consider consent freely given if the data subject has no genuine or free choice or cannot refuse or 'withdraw consent without detriment' (Lucente and Clark, 2020, p. 8). Finally, organisations that rely on and use personal data must, under Article 25, design ('bake') data protection measures into their processes by default in the assumption that this will offer the ultimate prophylactic against data breaches.

Notwithstanding, a general understanding across jurisdictions of the needs and rights of data subjects appears stronger in recent decades, even though not all jurisdictions refer to a 'data subject', all concern an individual to whom the data relates. Safeguarding, in that sense, assumes that character given to it by Luciano Floridi, namely, the protection of 'personal identity by data that are not arbitrary labels for, but rather constitutive traits of, the person in question' (2013, p. 249). Privacy laws are imprecise, however, and so space to disentangle privacy and data protection to allow for the separate consideration of personal data protection as a set of principles appears a less messy option. Niall MacDermot, the Conservative Member of Parliament for derby North, mooted this during the 1970 Right to Privacy Bill debate, where he said that, 'the problem of the data banks and computers is quite separate form that with which we have been dealing [the right to privacy]. It is exceedingly difficult', he concluded, 'and will need different legislation' (Hansard HC Deb. vol. 794 col. 956, 23 January 1970). In a similar vein, Roger Brownsword applauds the separation between privacy (Article 7) and data protection (Article 8) in the Charter of Fundamental Rights of the European Union (2019, p. 313). Whether a separation epitomised by the Charter really prevails with today's technologies and hybridised or compounded techno-social domains is debatable. Article 7 mentions communications, and whilst communication technologies take on a variety of forms, most involve personal data in ways that question not only issues of data protection but also of privacy, as those two exist in the Charter's scope. Conceived over twenty years ago, the Charter represents a world at once familiar and strange for being less replete with consumer technologies or fortified by the tyrannies of technologically mediated choice. Yet, GDPR sites the Charter in its introductory paragraph as the basis of the fundamental right for protecting natural persons in relation to the processing of personal data, a locus of understanding of data privacy that appears both immutable and rational.

In Europe and the United States there remains a dialogue, notably between the CCPA and GDPR, albeit one yet to find common ground on alignments of privacy and protection, nor a settled or considerable understanding of the data subject. Compared with the CCPA, GDPR, as already discussed, stresses protection over privacy, or perhaps more accurately the protection of individual rights over data rather than data protection *per se* (Warren and Dearnley, 2005, p. 239). This does not make privacy redundant for GDPR, but rather, as we have seen from legislative discussions stretching back decades, privacy is folded implicitly into GDPRs (prophylactic) vision, for example Recital 2, 'the protection of natural persons with regard to the processing of their personal data, whatever their nationality or residence', where 'their' functions as a reminder of the status of the individual as a bearer of rights enfolding privacy and allowing for claims where privacy is breached. Hence, GDPR appears to include privacy as an intuitive corollary of protection by making privacy claims easier against data controllers and processors who violate or assault a data subject's determiner, 'their'. This includes compensation from the controller or processor for a person who has suffered 'material or non-material damage' (Article 82(1)), where 'non-material' damage means compensation for distress and hurt feelings regardless of whether financial loss is apparent, a subtle but clear echo of Warren and Brandeis' recognition of 'the heightening of sensations which came with the advance of civilization' and their corresponding demand within a right to privacy for the legal recognition of 'thoughts, emotions, and sensations' (1890, p. 195). Although a decision in the Irish Court of Appeal shows that data subjects seeking access to 'their' data (i.e. a subject access request under Article 15 GDPR) are unlikely to get it. Instead, the decision in *Nowak v DPC* [2020] IECA 174, based on access requests defined by Article 12 of the Data Protection Directive 95/46/EC yet relevant to post-GDPR data controls because the definition of personal data remains consistent across the legislation, is entitled to a 'copy' of the data in an 'intelligible form', rather than the 'original' data itself.

Relying on human intuition to underpin privacy claims in technological domains is problematic, however. Three mixed reasons that speak from different sides of the cybernetic border, but equally to the finely balanced relationship between humanity and its beautiful machines, explain why. First, Joe Jacob argues that in many of the decisions we must make each day,

> we depend on intuition and what is called judgement. We never endeavour to compute all possibilities but even where we are at our most rational merely a few and from these determine our course of action. This is part of our humanity. Where what we decide is conditioned by the outpourings of a machine, and, worse, we are answerable to that machine for our judgement, then we lose something of our humanity in the process (1972, pp. 546–547).

Second, seemingly in contrast to Jacob, Byung-Chul Han argues, 'intuition does not represent a higher form of knowing; instead it represents something merely subjective – a stopgap compensating for the shortage of objective data' (2017, p. 58). Third, Peter Blume assumes a more regulated approach yet remains, like Jacob, sceptical: 'It is likely that most data subjects will not be able to utilise a strengthened legal position. Even if more rights than today were automatic (i.e. not presupposing an own initiative), it is doubtful that the average data subject will be able to guard his/her own interests and privacy. Empowerment may sound fine', Blume concludes, 'but it creates an illusion' (2015, p. 264). What these three positions show us again, is part of a larger and more fundamental problem faced by the law in its attempts, misguided or thankless perhaps, to provide transparency, choice, certainty, or clarity to persons, communities, data subjects, and so. If machines and objective data have wrested intuition (relating to privacy in this case but equally more broadly as well) from human hands – a point of difference between Jacob and Han – a primordial shift in our understanding of ourselves is underway. It is arguably a cliché that the partnership between humanity and technology is always developing but that we have reached a stage in which information and an unerring belief in power of the knowledge derived from it are the ultimate catalysts and drivers across the social spectrum, from individual behaviour to international organisation. As Helen Nissenbaum claims, 'default constraints on streams of information from us and about us seem to respond not to social, ethical, and political logic but to the logic of technical possibility' (2011, p. 34). This is the *datus quo*.

Conclusions

During this and the previous chapter I have set out the *datus* quo of personal data, the data subject, and ideas, policies, and practices lawmakers have struggled with, and developed to regulate and govern datafication and the technologies that facilitate massive datafication practices. 'Individuals, business and machines are generating enormous international flows of data in what has been, to date, a readily global digital economy', argue Anupam Chander and Martina Ferracane in World Economic Forum whitepaper (2019, p. 7). They conclude that governments in response, 'are grappling with the interplay between these international data flows and domestic policy objectives related to privacy, consumer protection, economics, cybersecurity, national security and law enforcement' (2019, p. 7). The chapters that follow will further interrogate the *datus* quo as a site in which lawmakers grapple with data flows and policies and technical logic and knowledge grow in stature. But also a site in which the data subject's fundamental act of giving continues as a link between ancient notions of data subjectivity (encompassing personal data) and present conceptualisations, notably legal, that at once generalise and totalise data subjectivity.

The discussion will move on to consider data subjectivity stemming not only from instrumental economic notions of raw materiality, from laws legitimisation of that position, or from principles of 'labour' that correspond to a comprehensive shedding and leaching of personal data by individuals who either do not recognise or ignore in their online engagements and interactions, a *giving of themselves* that, it is important to note, transcends the banal practices of sharing or exchange promoted by social networks as a habit-forming user retention devices. Instead, we will explore data subjectivity and personal data as objects, including data subjects as assemblages or compounds of personal data objects more than their pieces, and personal data objects that do not and need not relate to a person, 'natural' or otherwise, at all. Only to another personal data object. Both accounts, I will argue, radically transform normative definitions of the data subject by discrediting the premise of the data subject as the one to whom personal data relates. Before data subjectivity there is *being* in data, and this is where we turn to next.

Notes

1. It is important to briefly note that a distinction is made in law between personal and non-personal data, the former of which will not be discussed in this book. See, for example, Regulation (EU) 2018/1807 of the European Parliament and of the Council of 14 November 2018 on a framework for the free flow of non-personal data in the European Union, which came into effect on 28 May 2019.
2. https://ico.org.uk/ (accessed 14 April 2020).
3. Blockchains on smartphones create cryptophones, and the particular example of the Taiwanese manufacturer HTC is interesting, although there are a variety of smaller companies such as Sirin Labs and Krip also building customised cryptophones. HTC are one of the first companies to build a cryptophone that provides the user with on-board encryption and decryption capabilities for enhanced content and identity security and access to cryptocurrency exchanges for trading tokens. https://www.htcexodus.com/eu/ (accessed 19 February 2020).
4. In the debate on the Right to Privacy Bill in 1970, John Lee, the Labour Member of Parliament for Reading, highlighted three basic abuses of individual privacy needing protection: 'The first is intrusion into the home. The second is unauthorised intrusion by a third party into a person's work relationships or by somebody who is connected with his work but who uses improper or irregular methods to obtain information. The third is intrusion into a person's personal relationships, whether sexual or social, or personal habits, not merely in the home, but at large' (Hansard HC Deb. vol. 794 col. 948, 23 January 1970).
5. Arguably the post-enlightenment movement of which Hegel was part considered that 'something larger' to be the state, which is not

an obvious point of allegiance for collective action online (Hampson, 1990, p. 282).
6. https://www.un.org/en/universal-declaration-human-rights/ (accessed 30 March 2020).
7. https://nsarchive2.gwu.edu//NSAEBB/NSAEBB194/Document%2031. pdf (accessed 30 March 2020).
8. What I call here a 'contradictory' position was outlined by the court in the European decision in *Lindquist* Case C-101/01 [2003] I-13030:

> Measures taken by the Member States to ensure the protection of personal data must be consistent both with the provisions of Directive 95/46 and with its objective of maintaining a balance between freedom of movement of personal data and the protection of private life.

References

European Commission. 2010. *Communication from the Commission to the European Parliament, The Council, The Economic and Social Committee and the Committee of the Regions COM(2010) 609 Final.* https://eur-lex.europa.eu/LexUriServ/LexUriServ.do?uri=COM:2010:0609:FIN:EN:PDF (accessed 25 July 2020).

Arendt, Hannah. 2000. *The Portable Hannah Arendt.* Edited by Peter Baehr. London: Penguin.

Aristotle. 1992. *Politics.* Translated by T.A. Sinclair. Revised and Re-Presented by Trevor J. Saunders. London: Penguin Classics.

Barlow, John PerryJohn Perry. 1996. *A Declaration of the Independence of Cyberspace.* https://www.eff.org/cyberspace-independence (accessed 19 May 2020).

Becker, Marcel. 2019. Privacy in the Digital Age: Comparing and Contrasting Individual Versus Social Approaches Towards Privacy. *Ethics and Information Technology.* Vol. 21, pp. 307–317.

Benkler, Yochai. 2006. *The Wealth of Networks: How Social Production Transforms Markets and Freedom.* New Haven: Yale University Press.

Blume, Peter. 2015. The Data Subject. *European Data Protection Law Review.* Vol. 1, No. 4, pp. 258–264.

Brownsword, Roger. 2019. *Law, Technology and Society: Re-Imagining the Regulatory Environment.* Abingdon: Routledge.

Brownsword, Roger and Morag Goodwin. 2012. *Law and the Technologies of the Twenty-First Century.* Cambridge: Cambridge University Press.

Castells, Manuel. 2010. *The Rise of the Network Society.* 2nd Edition. Chichester: Wiley-Blackwell.

Chander, Anupam and Martina F. Ferracane. 2019. Chapter 1: Regulating cross-border data flows – domestic good practices. *Exploring International Data Flow Governance: Platform for Shaping the Future of Trade and Global Economic Interdependence.* World Economic Forum, Whitepaper (December). http://www3.weforum.org/docs/WEF_Trade_Policy_Data_Flows_Report.pdf (accessed 12 May 2020).

Durbin, J. 1979. Statistics and the Report of the Data Protection Committee. *Journal of the Royal Statistical Society, Series A.* Vol. 142, Part 3, pp. 299–306.

Floridi, Luciano. 2013. *The Ethics of Information.* Oxford: Oxford University Press.

Freude, Alvar and Trixy Freude. 2016. Echoes of History: Understanding German Data Protection. *Bertelsmann Foundation*, 1 October. https://www. bfna.org/research/echos-of-history-understanding-german-data-protection/ (accessed 12 May 2020).

Fuchs, Christian. 2016. *Reading Marx in the Information Age.* Abingdon: Routledge.

Hampson, Norman. 1990. *The Enlightenment: An Evaluation of Its Assumptions, Attitudes and Values.* London: Penguin.

Han, Byung-Chul. 2017. *Psychopolitics: Neoliberalism and New Technologies of Power.* Translated by Erik Butler. London: Verso.

Herian, Robert. 2018. *Regulating Blockchain: Critical Perspectives in Law and Technology.* Abingdon: Routledge.

Herian, Robert. 2020. Blockchain, GDPR, and Fantasies of Data Sovereignty. *Law, Innovation and Technology.* Vol. 12, No. 1, pp. 156–174.

Jacob, Joe. 1971. Your Life on Their Tapes. *Mental Health.* Vol. 30 (summer), pp. 19–20.

Jacob, Joe. 1972. Computers and Privacy – a British Answer. *Anglo-American Law Review.* Vol. 1, No. 4, pp. 544–552.

Johnson, David R. and David G. Post. 1996. Law and Borders: The Rise of Law in Cyberspace. *Stanford Law Review.* Vol. 48, No. May, pp. 1367–1402.

Jones, Meg Leta. 2018. Does Technology Drive Law? The Dilemma of Technological Exceptionalism in Cyberlaw. *Journal of Law, Technology & Policy.* Vol. 2018, No. 2, pp. 249–284.

Käll, Jannice. 2018. Blockchain Control. *Law and Critique.* Vol. 29, pp. 133–140.

Kupfer, Joseph. 1987. Privacy, Autonomy, and Self-Concept. *American Philosophical Quarterly.* Vol. 24, No. 1 (January), pp. 81–89.

Locke, John. 2013. *Two Treatises of Government.* Edited by Peter Laslett. Cambridge: Cambridge University Press.

Lucente, Kate and James Clark (eds.). 2020. *Data Protection Laws of the World (Full Handbook).* DLA Piper. https://www.dlapiperdataprotection.com/ system/modules/za.co.heliosdesign.dla.lotw.data_protection/functions/ handbook.pdf?country=all (accessed 30 March 2020).

Manski, Sarah and Ben Manski. 2018. No Gods, No Masters, No Coders? The Future of Sovereignty in a Blockchain World. *Law and Critique.* Vol. 29, pp. 151–162.

Miller, Arthur R. 1971. *The Assault on Privacy: Computers, Data Banks, and Dossiers.* Ann Arbor, MI: The University of Michigan Press.

Morozov, Evgeny. 2014. *To Save Everything, Click Here: Technology, Solutionism and the Urge to Fix Problems That Don't Exist.* London: Penguin.

Morsink, Johannes. 1984. The Philosophy of the Universal Declaration. *Human Rights Quarterly.* Vol. 6, No. 3 (August), pp. 309–334.

Nissenbaum, Helen. 2011. A Contextual Approach to Privacy Online. *Daedalus, the Journal of the American Academy of Arts & Sciences.* Vol. 140, No. 4 (Fall), pp. 32–48.

Parent, W.A. 1983. Privacy, Morality, and the Law. *Philosophy and Public Affairs.* Vol. 12, pp. 269–288.

Parker, Richard B. 1974. A Definition of Privacy. *Rutgers Law Review.* Vol. 27, pp. 275–297.

Piketty, Thomas. 2014. *Capital in the Twenty-First Century.* Translated by Arthur Goldhammer. Cambridge: The Belknap Press of Harvard University Press.

Posner, Eric A. and E. Glen Weyl. 2018. *Radical Markets: Uprooting Capitalism and Democracy for a Just Society.* Princeton, NJ: Princeton University Press.

Regan, Priscilla M. 1984. Personal Information Policies in the United States and Britain: The Dilemma of Implementation Considerations. *Journal of Public Policy.* Vol. 4, No. 1, pp. 19–38.

Rees, Christopher. 2013. Tomorrow's Privacy: Personal Information as Property. *International Data Privacy Law.* Vol. 3, No. 4, pp. 220–221.

Rider, Priscilla L. 1959. Legal Protection of the Manifestations of Individual Personality – The Identity-Indicia. *Southern California Law Review*, Vol. 33, pp. 31–70.

Schoeman, Ferdinand. 1984. Privacy: Philosophical Dimension. *American Philosophical Quarterly.* Vol. 21, No. 3, pp. 199–213.

Spiekermann, Sarah, Alessandro Acquisti, Rainer Böhme and Kai-Lung Hui. 2015. The Challenges of Personal Data Markets and Privacy. *Electronic Markets.* Vol. 25, No. 2, pp. 161–167.

Tapper, Colin. 1977. Computers and Privacy. *The Modern Law Review.* Vol. 40, No. 2 (March), pp. 198–200.

Thomson, Judith Jarvis. 1975. The Right to Privacy. *Philosophy and Public Affairs.* Vol. 4, pp. 295–314.

Warren, Adam and James Dearnley. 2005. Data Protection Legislation in the United Kingdom: From Development to Statute 1969–84. *Information, Communication & Society.* Vol. 8, No. 2, pp. 238–263.

Warren, Samuel D. and Louis D. Brandeis. 1890. The Right to Privacy. *Harvard Law Review*, Vol. 4, No. 5 (December 15), pp. 193–220.

Willis, Sarah. 1994. Data Privacy or Protection? The Data Subject's Interest. *Law, Computers & Artificial Intelligence.* Vol. 3, No. 1, pp. 67–83.

3   Being in data

Introduction

Following the outline and some tentative criticism of the *datus quo* in the last two chapters, I turn now to philosophy and theory to interrogate personal data and the data subject as ontological phenomena. This means *being in data*: an essence and an excess that precedes the instrumental configuration of humanity determined as the one to whom data relates, that indelible and ubiquitous relationship of person and data from which a bundle of legal and economic qualities known as data subjectivity – natural, protected, private persons, etc. – and data sovereignty emerge. As Richard Powers says in his novel *The Overstory*, 'Petabytes of airborne messages swarm all around in the air. They collect in sensors and bounce off satellites. They stream from the cameras now mounted in every building and on each intersection' (2018, p. 605). This is a relationship which is traceable and trackable as an aesthetic form such as a 'data visualisation' but never certain as to its boundaries or knowable as legal, political, or economic (statistical) truths. This chapter and the next will deal with two main themes by encompassing positions including the phenomenology and existentialism of Heidegger, the object-orientated ontology (OOO), immaterialism, and speculative realism of Graham Harman, Jane Bennett, Timothy Morton, and Ian Bogost.

First, I will discuss being concerning *dataness* both in terms of the data subject and of personal data. What, in Heideggerian terminology, I call *da(ta)sein*, a configuration of being with data appearing at its core. Although, as I argue later in this chapter, being is not a fixed configuration but contingent upon our present historical stage of political economy, neoliberal capitalism, a particular contextualisation of being I accept that Heidegger would be unlikely to agree with. Second, I will discuss the 'relationship' between the data subject and personal data not as a taken-for-granted condition privileging legal right or economic reason – the ability for the one to whom data relates to emerge as an enlightened economic or legal subjectivity – but as the withdrawal, failure, and (re)emergence of bonds and tensions between those subjectivities and data regarded to be personal as different objects that withhold from each other and from those observing them. Central to the following discussion is the possibility or actuality of a separation between the data and subject, not in a traditional Cartesian object/subject dichotomy, but as two objects that withdraw from, relate to one another, yet never attain a total unity that allows us (observers, data analysts, etc.) to point with absolute clarity and certainty at the one to whom data relates. What I am suggesting here is radical in the sense that that it attempts to push past what Timothy Morton calls the '*transcendental* gap' between a thing and how it appears, its data (2018, p. 22). For me, data ought not simply or only to be thought of as 'thing-data' – data that is indistinguishably related to *its* thing, such as personal data to *its* subject – but as objects in their own right, although not necessarily or automatically with the legal connotations that might imply. We will consider this withdrawal in more depth in the next chapter using some examples. But setting the scene now is important.

Private and public organisations collect massive amounts of personal data to piece together pictures of individuals and communities. The purpose of data is to construct reliable (de-risked) and efficacious models of consumer choice and behaviour. More than that, it makes consumers complicit in models that reflect co-functional openings to freedom, injunctions to love data, and assignments of, as Jean Baudrillard states, 'a place in the overall economic order' (1996, p. 152). Roberto Simanowski talks of data love as 'a phenomenon not only of the society of control but also of the consumer society. And data love thrives on precisely the same data that security and privacy would claim to protect' (2016, p. xiii). On this basis of consumer conditioning and orientation, I argue that data assumes the legally and culturally potent 'personal' status. Personalisation, argues Baudrillard, is 'a basic ideological concept of a society which 'personalizes' objects and beliefs solely in order to integrate persons more effectively' (1996, p. 152). But neither the object 'data subject' nor the object(s) 'personal data' reveal or express full proof, authentic or genuine truths, either of reason or fact to those that require them to do so, whether for economic reasons or any other reason. Such truths remain stubbornly hidden no matter how detailed and fine-grained the picture of me, you, them, or us appears to be.[1] The object 'data subject', as an analogue of the object 'one to who data relates' conditioned to give up and give out valuable data, withdraws from attempts to know it by 'their' data. The object 'personal data' also withdraws on its own account but with the same effects of triggering greater demand and belief in the value of data.

Legally, and, to a large extent, culturally we consider these two objects indivisible. When a person, protected in law by their status as 'data subject', seeks redress from commercial or government actors for policies that threaten the privacy of 'my' data, the data and its subject are always already a self-supporting evidentiary unity. As Luciano Floridi maintains, " 'My' in 'my information' is not the same 'my' as in 'my car' but rather the same 'my' as in 'my body' or 'my feelings': it expresses a sense of constitutive *belonging*, not of external *ownership*, a sense in which my body, my feelings, and my information are part of me but are not my (legal) possessions" (2013, p. 244). The instinct, therefore, is to pursue legal or ethical protections rooted in the actuality of this unity, regardless of a breakdown in the clarity or certainty of that characterisation. Hence, you end up with problematic statements that acknowledge the messiness of data but seek redemption in the certainty of the 'data subject', such as,

> As the product of multiple sites of work, layered analytic techniques, experimental practices, and various competing discourses, Big Data are susceptible to losing provenance and their ability to be "about" only one thing, their origins and interpretations becoming multiple and conflicting as metadata are mixed with primary secondary, and derivative data. Such a confluence of data sources and meanings inevitably leads to data disorder, the potential for harm to data subjects, and the need for strong ethical investigations into data and its discontents.
>
> (Iliadis and Russo, 2016, p. 2)

Business models built on data scraping, harvesting, and extraction do not struggle with notions of separation or separating a subject from data as an actual undercurrent of 'depersonalisation' driving the ideological narratives of 'personalization' mentioned by Baudrillard. Corporate consumer loyalty strategies and brand affiliations massaged by sophisticated marketing and advertising campaigns seek to convince individuals of deep, personal relationships between them and the product on sale (i.e. anything from trainers to first-class airline travel). Yet all the while working with models that refuse to accord data with the subject. Depersonalisation is not an unfamiliar process for businesses, where it enables leveraging of economic advantages. This strategy has been widespread in capitalist societies for decades. It is, for example, the depersonalisation that Arthur Davidson, the Labour Member of Parliament for Accrington speaking in the debate on the Control of Personal Information Bill in 1972, envisaged when he argued that, 'instead of the computer picture being like me, I tend to become like the computer picture' (Hansard HC Deb. vol. 835 col. 1004, 21 April 1972). More recent commentators have referred to this as data doubling, but with much the same effect. 'The data double highlights both the negative space between an individual and their digital representation, and how the position and intention of the analyst influences how the double is constructed, what is included or left out and what kinds of action it is shaped to facilitate', argue Dalton *et al.*, concluding that big data 'exaggerates this otherness because its origins are commercial and it necessitates new tools and approaches, which in turn can be better monetized if the data is also opaque in terms of meaning' (2016, p. 4). The human being to whom data relates is only secondary, even subservient, to 'their' data in the eyes of data-orientated business models that prefer the machine-readable value, efficiency, and ease of persons manifesting 'like the computer picture' of them.

Separating or distinguishing the personal from the data (or from 'its' data) aims at removing the messy unpredictability of humans. This obfuscates, if not eliminates, the nature and range of responsibilities, duties, and liabilities on businesses (and governments that use the same process logics), while lowering costs and improving efficiency, which is the goal. It is the case that General Data Protection Regulation (GDPR) and Californian Consumer Privacy Act (CCPA) have reinstated or rather redistributed through the data controller/ subject relationship some responsibilities, duties, and liabilities back onto the shoulders of business and government, but this has not stopped a general trend in depersonalisation as a commercial strategy or governance policy. These processes, policies, and strategies are not ignorant of the fact that, at a fundamental level, the value of the data lies in its personality, so to speak, and what defines it as 'personal', where personality shows actual or potential purchasing, voting and consuming habits and behaviours in an individual or targeted cohort. Depersonalisation remains key, however. The practice of anonymisation, considered vital to protecting data subjects, is, I argue, a logical conclusion to economic strategies of depersonalisation, where it represents a willing commitment, by business, government, and data subject alike, to uncouple that messy humanity from its valuable kernel.

A growing hunger for personal data in the wake of Covid-19 may show us the further interesting and heightened influence of anonymisation.

The concept of being allows, as far as is possible, to 'get under the skin' of personal data and data subjectivity as interrelated yet different and separate objects. The focus on being does not unite or attempt to unite personal data with 'its' subject but refers instead to both as objects of ontological interest. This is not the end of my analysis, however. Politically, being in data spotlights individualism as an inherent and unassailable neoliberal capitalist precept cast in the contemporary form of data subjectivity, one based on the primacy of personal data's economic value by the likes of GDPR and CCPA. Regardless of stipulations in GDPR for subject access rights there is and can be, I argue, no individual command, control, or sovereignty over personal data by the data subject in the *datus quo* not already accounted for by governments or businesses staking a claim to it as an inviolable source or raw material for their sole benefit, advantage, or gratification. There are plenty of ways to sell ideas and promises of command, control, and sovereignty over personal data to individuals, but each is as disingenuous as the last when, as Roberto Simanowski points out, 'We are on a mission to produce data ceaselessly and in perpetuity' (2016, p. xii). Economic demands and requirements that give structure to and provide meaning for the activities of data subjects on- and even offline always already define what data subjectivity is. Put another way, the data subject exists but only as a masquerade, yet another veiled species of capitalist subjectivity. In the *datus quo* there are no data subjects only economic subjects, and law's role is to legitimate their 'free', 'fair', and 'private' existence in cyberspace and vouchsafe the abundance of their free-flowing personal data to a variety of stakeholders. Being in data suggests something different, however. It punctuates the smooth exterior of this neoliberal capitalist discourse and the universal definition of lawmakers of personal data regimes with alternative positions on data subjectivity and ethics.

Further, it provides an alternative viewpoint on the notion that if businesses and governments want 'our' personal data they must pay for it. Some commentators may deem this common sense, but it is nothing more than a further capitulation of being to the depersonalising tendencies of economy and markets. Market-socialist models are fantasies of post-capitalist data sovereignty that only confirm the pre-eminence of economic not data subjectivity (Posner and Weyl, 2018). Market socialism involving or requiring an array of different self-directed technological 'solutions' and applications does not reverse or even problematise the depersonalisation caused by datafication practices. Instead, market socialism promotes, amongst other things, that we abrogate all bonds and tensions of human inter-relatedness, what we might call ethics or politics, to markets. The 'socialism' annexed to these markets ideals is a non-sequitur that does not warrant serious attention, let alone comment. Socialism itself has long ceased to be an effective foil against capitalism in many respects (Žižek, 2009; Bosteels, 2014). We will return to look at some of these models and supporting technologies, or rather problems with them, as we consider potential or rather speculative actualities of data sub-jectivity beyond the *datus quo* in the next chapter. Now I want to turn to the key theoretical framing of my understanding of being in data.

Da(ta)sein

Following Heidegger to this initial discussion of being in data means, as the heading of this section suggests, leaving behind (temporarily, at least) any distinction between personal and non-personal data as the two basic categories to which the fate of data subjects align within the *datus quo*. It also means leaving behind (again, temporarily) the subjec-tivity of the data subject as, in Heidegger's philosophy – notably, *Being and Time* – a bogus conflation of 'the first- and third-person points of view' and a false promise of 'a perfectly harmonized unity of perspec-tives' that would show individual reason concerning, consciousness of, or sovereignty over object data (Heidegger, 1996; Carman, 2007, p. 292). Rather than subjects perceiving objects in the world, Heidegger regarded people (if subjects at all) as being (*Dasein*) *in* and *amongst* the world, amongst objects *within* the world that the traditional philoso-phies of Descartes and Kant, and even to some extent the philosophies of his direct phenomenological predecessors Hegel and Husserl, could not fathom without intervention from human perception, observations, or consciousness. Unlike Descartes' ego determination of the world, Heidegger does not consider a world inferred by the contents of the individual mind, as the sole property of the subject as an observer, but *Dasein* starts in the world and is essentially in it. For Heidegger, there-fore, being is a fundamental form of coping: *Dasein* undertakes a series of practical steps and activities in the familiar environs of its world that are largely or entirely transparent, meaning such activities do not reg-ister in consciousness because no aspect of the activity demands it. Put another way, as beings we only become conscious of objects within the world when aspects of them disturb or intrude upon consciousness at which point, we rationalise those objects and attempt to solve the world to the detriment of an authentic meaning and significance of *Dasein*.

Data-sein and *dataness* point to a radical departure from the *datus quo*, therefore, because of the ontological situatedness of the person to whom data relates; and the 'whatness' concerning the question of essence – essence being what the thing is considered to be – and, therefore, the essence of data as a universal or inclusive genus 'data' that precedes personal and non-personal differentiation as rationalisations or attempts to order and solve the world and being in data, but which cannot always do so (Heidegger, 2011, p. 233). But this is in many respects a conclusion and thus the wrong place to begin. Not least because it also takes beyond Heidegger to the more recent philosophical position known as OOO, where one of the key proponents, Ian Bogost, reminds us that 'For Martin Heidegger, objects *are* outside human consciousness, but their *being* exists only in human understanding', a position that OOO disregards because of the reducibility of objects it attributes to Heidegger's thinking (2012, p. 4). We will return to OOO later. The work of Heidegger's that I refer to here is not, in the main, *Being and Time*, but his short essay 'The Question Concerning Technology', an important if flawed account of man's relationship with what Heidegger refers to as modern technology. Flawed where Heidegger uses a paucity of examples to illustrate his questioning of technology, and while those he offers and relies upon are commendable in their simplicity, they appear to tell us very little about our hyper-technical world or the befuddling complexities of the Information Age. In defence of Heidegger, however, I do not think his lack of examples nor their simplicity matter all that much. What he provides instead is a pure descriptive and analytic method – a phenomenology – that is ahistorical, de-contextualised yet translatable and interpretable into the terms of today's technological world, if we accept the challenge of doing so.

Flawed also because of an ahistorical, pasteurised character to Heidegger's philosophy. The work I focus on here, for example, says little of anything, at least not expressly, about the political, economic, legal, or cultural significance of technology, nor does he speak of ethics concerning technology. Again, if we accept Heidegger's challenge to question technology, then socialising Heidegger's philosophy for the present moment by putting it to work in and on today's technosocial contexts is ours to do. Way-markers that point to political, economic, cultural, legal significance are abundant in Heidegger's essay if we care to look. Perhaps Heidegger's own misadventures with the politics of national socialism during Hitler's Third Reich would suggest taking care when summoning the political in his work. This is not the place to discuss or debate this matter, although it remains pertinent given the subject of this book, if we take seriously that there were links between Heidegger's theory of technology and his brief foray into national socialism (Rockmore, 1992; Wolin, 1998). However, I remain convinced by Heidegger's importance to the Western philosophical tradition, especially regarding his articulations of being and essence, and fall-back on the benefit gained from using what I need from it in the present discussion. As John Caputo states, 'You ignore Heidegger at your peril. His influence reaches into nearly every corner of contemporary arts and culture. as maddening as this is to many, he remains the dominant figure of twentieth-century continental philosophy – and there is no way around him' (2018, p. 30).

There is another important and perhaps obvious point which I need to touch on before going further. This book is about personal data and the data subject and here I am proposing an essay on questioning technology, not questioning data. We know data and technology relate to one another. Throughout the book I have given examples of technologies and how they correspond with, generate, rely upon, and use data. But common-sense says most people would not consider data technology, at least not in the way they would consider a computer, smart phone, car, lawnmower, or satellite orbiting Earth technologies. Rather, data is something separate from the technologies that measure, sense, generate, digitise, store, and manage it. If an eyeball is a technology, the colour, shape, and movement of objects that the eyeball observes and perceives are the data sent to the brain for configuration into meaning, impartible information, and knowledge. Therefore, we can divide data and technology into separate camps. I believe the distinction between data and technology is not this binary or clear-cut, although not because I believe data is a technology. Far from evading the matter by not answering the issue here and now, I believe the relevance to data (personal data and the data subject) of Heidegger's question of technology will become clear as we work our way through the key features of his essay. Another way to look at it is to say that focusing on data helps bring Heidegger's essay into the twenty-first century and refine it for contemporary tastes, because as we live in time of technologies, our moment in the Information Age has brought information, and by extension data, to equal if not greater prominence.

The Question Concerning Technology begins with Heidegger bemoaning the effects of modern technology on mankind where it 'makes us utterly blind to the essence of technology' (2011, pp. 217–218). Passages such as 'Everywhere we remain unfree and chained to technology, whether we passionately affirm or deny it' resonate with the present historical stage of the Information Age, a commercial techno-sociality dominated by unwavering adherence to personal devices, social media, e-commerce, digital literacy, and, perhaps above all, the production, dissemination, storage, and commodification of data. Of particular concern in Heidegger's definition of modern technology, as distinct from pre-modern 'handicraft' technologies, are questions of instrumentality, of technology as a means to an end for human activity, and how this imposes upon revealing the essence of technology as anything but technological or concerning what we would consider technological objects. This leads Heidegger to an 'instrumental and anthropological definition of technology', although this is an insufficient definition both for Heidegger and at present (2011, p. 218). Rather, the correctness of treating technology only as instrumental to human activity unravels in the face of what Heidegger calls 'the will to mastery', whereby 'everything depends on our manipulating technology in the proper manner as a means' and 'becomes all the more urgent the more technology threatens to slip from human control' (2011, p. 218).

Here we catch our first glimpse of why this essay is significant to our questioning of data. Data, I argue, more obviously slips from human control daily under the forces driving the datus quo than technologies do. Control has, for a long time, occupied the discourse of lawmakers and privacy advocates. Data controllers, for instance, assume god-like control in the form of oversight of the purposes and means of personal data processing (Article 4.7, GDPR). The will to mastery, therefore, is a key indicator of why there is a growing human devotion to technology across a broad spectrum of instrumentality – from the grandiose science of Conseil Européen pour la Recherche Nucléaire (CERN) to cordless lawnmowers. With modern technologies humanity seeks to tame, observe, and command what it calls 'nature' – that perpetual *other* to the rational integrity of the individual self – although not always in that order. Data emissions from every conceivable object known to nature have been key to humanity achieving this level of mastery, and more data, we are told, can only enhance mastery of nature further. A growing majority of networked technologies today need data to provide this mastery (or illusions of it). The Internet of Things (IoT) is a prime example of this, whereby individuals and their devices (e.g. a 'smart fridge') collaborate to produce valuable personal data not, as Nick Couldry and Andreas Hepp maintain, to improve the device or tool in question, but 'to enable us to be better targeted by advertisers and marketers' (2017, p. 131). Many deviceswith the prefix 'smart' generate and draw upon data that contribute to cross-fertilising ecommerce and various forms of online surveillance. Will to mastery on these terms is, therefore, mastery of consumer will, choice, and behaviour, including mastery of what David Lyon, following Shoshana Zuboff, refers to as 'behavioural surplus' or the 'the mundane, everyday data that our machines exude constantly' (2019, p. 68). This would be a more narrowly defined consideration – online retail is, after all, not everything in life – but for the interlocking of consumerism and datafication in the construction and surveillance of all modes of social life and being today. As a result, we find the same will to mastery of the corresponding will, choice, and behaviour of an individual as consumer – or more likely 'prosumer', a semantic work-around to stave off accusations of individual passivity[2] – regardless of whether we are discussing retention and progression of university students, voter apathy, credit scoring, or the location and movements of potential virus spreaders. Data analytics levels all forms of social life, and for any individual, organisation or institution to thrive, all must comply.

Mastery becomes even more urgent for businesses when the messiness of humanity is untamed by its own rationalising technologies and algorithms deployed for the purpose and (ironically) cannot correspond with statistical models and calculations built from massive datasets. To paraphrase the quote from Labour parliamentarian Arthur Davidson at the start of this chapter: mastery becomes more urgent when I tend to become less like, or unlike, the computer picture of me.[3] In that event, modelling deems more data necessary to bring the picture of me (back) into sharper focus and data controllers must work harder and more vociferously at achieving this, including through innovation of computational and algorithmic forms and processes to improve the chances of knowing or guessing me better by making my picture clearer. Here we touch upon the casual link Heidegger makes 'wherever instrumentality reigns', a four-fold causation comprising *causa materialis*, the material or the matter out of which something is made; *causa formalis*, the form or the shape into which the material enters; *causa finalis*, the end to which the form is put, that determines its use based on form and matter; and the *causa efficiens*, that which brings about the effect that it is a finished, actual, form (2011, p. 219). Heidegger's own example used to illustrate these four causative types concerns a silver chalice and the silversmith who fashions it. His example, therefore, concerns tangible, physical material easy to imagine in terms of everyday perception. We might not have access to a silver chalice, but we know what a metal beaker or cup looks like. Also, we have experience of how it feels to the touch on a hot or cold day, how it reflects the light at different times of the day, and so on.

There are, I suggest, several ways that we can interpret these four causative types concerning data, yet the digital domains in which we find ourselves are not tactile but ethereal and difficult to grasp objects within, as we would grasp a metal cup from a table in a room. Following the Davidson example (or rather my paraphrasing of it), we might consider the *materialis* as datum or bits of data gathered to make the computer picture of me. The picture of me is the form the data takes, the digitalised *formalis*, which we might also call information where it is a processed form of the data that stands apart from the physical embodiment of me as a human being. As Meredith Hoy maintains concerning the cybernetic turn from the mid-twentieth century, which I also associate with the *datus quo*, 'the world becomes understood in terms of data, which, when organized into intelligible patterns, become information. Every phenomenon, from the structuring of matter to the firing of neurons, is reducible to the production of informatic signals' (2018, p. 302). However, we should not discount the data subject as *formalis*, where it represents a legal status or condition of right with data processing that accords with a breach of privacy or confidence. While we are told, by the likes of GDPR for instance, that we are all data subjects, this means little until things go wrong and we seek to enforce our rights and gain redress from the courts. We can see, because of a causation of form analysis, therefore, different qualities in the division between a person or 'one to whom data relates', what I consider here as the primordial generator of data, compared with the data subject as a legal subject wronged by reckless, malicious, or negligent handling and processing of data by data controllers and brought into being (legal being). In sum, a person gives out data gathered up and mishandled by an organisation, at which point the data results back to the person now as data subject, as a bearer of rights, to enable law to perform and make good on its promise of restitution.

What determines the form of the picture of or information concerning me, and thus the *finalis*? I suggest, foremost, that this takes us back to the point I made earlier concerning the interlocking of consumerism and datafication in the present moment of Information Age. In the nineteenth century the ends to which stakeholders subjected data would not have amounted to very much overall, although it varied based on issues of class and race, for example. The collection of data and information on most of the population was limited to the census. Fine-grained personal information, so valuable to advertisers today, was not available. The Hollerith system, discussed in Chapter 2, showed the efficiency demanded from technology for quickly counting large numbers of people but prevented more information than would fit within the four corners of a punch-card. Such systems captured all life, but not being. Several countries did not count people in black, brown, indigenous, or immigrant communities in the same way, if at all. Whereas, if you were a member of middle-class or high society (like Warren and Brandeis, for example) your 'picture' had much higher value beyond census data, including the burgeoning sensationalist press, thus prompting you to write a lengthy discourse on the right to privacy of your 'picture' when you felt it was under threat.

Today, as we have seen, the story is very different. The *causa finalis* of individual information interests many different stakeholders looking for commercial and non-commercial (i.e. government) surveillance. Or, rather, we can short-circuit the variety of interests and say that the *causa finalis* of individual information is surveillance. We generate data for and because surveillance demands it of us, much like the example of IoT mentioned earlier and something that takes on new meaning in our emerging, post-pandemic world of 'track of trace'. Further, if we reconsider the definition of data controllers in Article 4.7 of GDPR – 'controller means the natural or legal person, public authority, agency or other body which, alone or jointly with others, determines the purposes and means of the processing of personal data; where the purposes and means of such processing are determined by Union or Member State law, the controller or the specific criteria for its nomination may be provided for by Union or Member State law' [emphasis added] – use of the term 'determine' stands out as a deliberate correlation between data controllers and data processing, of which surveillance, including surveillance capitalism, is a significant beneficiary within the datus quo. Surveillance capitalism, as a prominent type, is thus an end (*finalis*) which determines information, and by extension both the *materialis* and *formalis*, on Heidegger's account. Further, Heidegger's silver chalice example is determined to a sacrificial rite, and I make a similar claim as to personal data in the following chapter, with specific reference to what I call data 'tonsure', a data market-driven rite that echoes the sacrificial cutting of hair in India often sold to make wigs and hair weaves in the United States (Heidegger, 2011, p. 219).

The *causa efficiens*, which in Heidegger's example is the silversmith, leads us to the one that brings about the effect that is the finished, actual 'picture'. Again, the digital realm of my 'picture' compared with the realms of handicraft and artisans that interest Heidegger does not point to an individual, such as a silversmith, responsible for the finished effect of the 'picture'. The finished effect of my 'picture' is likely to be computational or algorithmic and thus free from prolonged human intervention, interest, or even control. Against a backdrop of what he calls 'runaway data', Frank Pasquale argues that 'Critical decisions are made not on the basis of the data per se, but on the basis of data analysed algorithmically: that is, in calculations coded in computer software' (2015, pp. 21–22). People provide algorithms with data as a silversmith is provided with silver. One produces a silver chalice, the other information or a 'picture' of, amongst other things, consumer behaviour patterns. Data controllers, as we have seen, relate to *causa finalis* rather than *efficiens*, despite having oversight of data processing, which might otherwise be akin to the silversmith fashioning a chalice.

But there is, I suggest, a further twist to the *causa efficiens* of information that involves trends in data sovereignty, which I have described elsewhere in terms of neoliberal governmentality, and which introduce political economy in a way Heidegger would not (Herian, 2020). Here the primordial one to whom data relates, as a person prior to the status of data subject is, I suggest, a good candidate for *efficiens*. However, unlike Heidegger's silversmith, there are, with people and data, obvious overlaps between the material, the form, and the one who brings about the finished effect of data in the case of the one to whom data relates. A silversmith does not generate the silver for the chalice either from their bodily person or because of having 'silver' in their title. Yet, that is what the one to whom data relates does. But Heidegger distinguishes between the silversmith as finisher of the actual, not the sacrificial chalice. In making this distinction he highlights three co-responsible ways that make the chalice a sacrificial vessel: matter (*hyle*), which is the silver; aspect (eidos), the sacred vessel indebted to chaliceness; and bounds (telos), which circumscribes the chalice as a sacrificial vessel by confining it to the realm of consecration and bestowal (Heidegger, 2011, p. 220). As finisher of the actual chalice, the silversmith is, therefore, co-responsible for the sacrificial vessel but is not a *causa efficiens* of the sacrificial vessel. This is because, Heidegger tells us, the silversmith does not bring about 'the finished sacrificial chalice as if it were the effect of a making' (2011, p. 220). The silversmith does not possess the power or authority to make the silver chalice anything other than a silver chalice, to circumscribe it with telos. Instead, Heidegger argues, 'The silversmith considers carefully and gathers together the three aforementioned ways of being responsible and indebted' (2011, p. 220). 'To consider carefully [*überlegen*]', he continues, 'is in Greek *legein*, *logos*. *Legein* is rooted in *apophainesthai*, to bring forward into appearance', concluding, therefore, that the 'silversmith is co-responsible as that from which the scared vessel's

being brought forth and subsistence take and retain their first departure' (Heidegger, 2011, p. 220).

As data sovereigns, ones to whom data relates bring forward into
appearance their own 'pictures'. Within neoliberal governmentality,
this bringing forward assumes the character of a rational choice by
an entrepreneurial self-transforming 'in more market-friendly direction', for fostering markets in 'pictures' and engaging in a risk game
of reward or failure (Mirowski, 2014, p. 127). 'A denizen of modern
neoliberal society has not demonstrated real flexibility of personal
identity until they have prostrated themselves before the capricious
god of risk', argues Philip Mirowski, freedom without 'the uninhib-
ited embrace of risk cannot be experienced as anything other than
static mechanical "choice". Any machine can achieve that. Salvation
through the market', he concludes, 'comes not from solidarity with
any delusional social class or occupational category, but instead bold
assertion of individuality through capitulation to a life of risk' (2014,
p. 120). Co-responsible for finishing a 'picture' of themselves, data
sovereigns consider carefully and gather together data in a valuable
aspect of information indebted to it, accounting for both as a comple-
tion and settlement of the productive value of information (telos). In
short, neoliberal data sovereigns bring forward into appearance a final,
marketable 'picture' of themselves conditioned by market acceptance
under the assumption of financial reward. Yet another way to view
this is that data uses us rather than us using the data. Data sovereigns,
therefore, do not bring forward into appearance their own 'picture'
or data double, the 'picture' speaks a truth about the data sovereign.
Contra Heidegger, Hubert Dreyfus maintains, this represents a society based on a system 'that no one directs but that moves toward the
total mobilization and enhancement of all beings' (1993, p. 306). For
Heidegger 'the perfectly ordered society dedicated to the welfare of all
is not the solution to our problems but the culmination of the technological understanding of being', a description that at once recalls and
condemns a broad spectrum of modern techno-solutionist tendencies,
from infectious Silicon Valley idealism to the more ideologically targeted concepts such as 'fully automated luxury communism' (Bastani,
2019).

If this were not the process of personal data monetisation attractive to many today via Web 2.0 services and platforms, we might
think it a parody of data sovereignty based on a 'Wanted' poster in a
Western movie.[4] As a report by the global consultancy firm McKinsey
& Company proclaims: 'People from all segments and geographies are
spending numerous hours online, publishing huge amounts of data.

Never before has so much unbiased and timely information been available for those able to translate data into a basis for making commercial decisions' (p. 1). Or, as Roberto Simanowski puts it: 'We live in an information society. And we love it!' (2016, p. xii) Here the reward for the 'Wanted' is in surrendering oneself, rather than being caught by a posse. Like Heidegger's silversmith, a data sovereign does not possess the power or authority to demand or advocate use of their 'picture' particularly, despite their supposed 'sovereignty'. Both a silversmith in bringing to appearance a sacred vessel and data sovereigns bringing to appearance data and information perform vital services on behalf of higher orders of authority and power, be it the Christian Church (silversmith) or neoliberal capitalism (data sovereigns). Both are also 'responsible', a key word for Heidegger that he describes as 'starting something on its way into arrival', an 'occasioning or an inducing to go forward [*Ver-an-lassen*]' (2011, p. 221). Data sovereigns are, however, marked by their association to 'their picture' in ways that a silversmith is not the *causa efficiens* of the chalice as a sacrificial vessel, and bring about the finished 'picture' as if were the effect of a making. Further, data sovereigns combine a mechanical bringing forth into appearance involving the 'arising of something from out of itself' (*physis*), with what Heidegger otherwise reserves for non-artisanal work such as that of the silversmith, a poetic bringing forth into appearance of the artisan (*poiēis*).

For Heidegger, bringing forth does not reach ultimate conclusions regarding essence – it does not uncover or reveal dataness. But technology as a way of revealing is critical to revealing as truth and Heidegger makes the connection, initially, between technology and technē as the name 'not only for the activities and skills of craftsman but also for the arts of the mind and the fine arts' (2011, p. 222). Technology, or pre-modern technology, reveals but does not manufacture. For Heidegger, pre-modern and modern technologies, distinguished by the exactness of science in the latter, vary in their bringing forth as poetic. As if taking Heidegger at his word, in a special report on managing information published in 2010, The Economist referred to a new profession, data scientist, as one 'who combines the skills of software programmer, statistician and storyteller/artist to extract the nuggets of gold hidden under mountains of data' (p. 4). In contrast to pre-modern technology, modern technology 'challenges' as a basis of its revealing, meaning putting to nature the unreasonable demand, in Heidegger's mind, that it supplies energy 'which can be extracted and stored as such' (2011, p. 223). On this basis we can return to my evaluation of data sovereigns given a moment ago, as combiners of poetic and physical bringing forth; we are all expected to be data scientists, albeit unskilled and unqualified ones. We can hold neoliberal influence responsible for data sovereigns as purgatorial stations of being hovering between primordial ones to whom data relates and legally accounted for data subjects, although law or one's realising of legal right does not guarantee freedom from neoliberalism. The role of law and regulation instead maintains one as data subject in condition of subservience to the economic reasoning of efficiency and growth pegged to data proliferation.

Neoliberalism has tracked across society in lockstep with the rise of data as a valuable resource in the last forty years of the Information Age and fostered strategies that survey, constantly, that which can be extracted and stored. This points towards an essence of data sovereignty and data subjectivity as indistinguishable from neoliberal being. Data subjectivity and sovereignty are the truth or the 'correctness of representation' of neoliberal being (Heidegger, 2011, p. 222). We are, as beings in neoliberalism, data subjects, if not always data sovereigns, willing and able to give up and give out data in many extractive practices for short, medium, and long-term storage. For Hubert Dreyfus, this realisation of the fate of human being, as discouraging or encouraging as it may be, is central to Heidegger's questioning of technology and thus offers us something on the matter of data, I suggest. '[A]lthough our understanding of things and ourselves as resources to be ordered, enhanced, and used efficiently has been building up since Plato', Dreyfus argues, 'we are not stuck with that understanding', and he continues,

> Although the technological understanding of being governs the way things have to show up for us, we can be open to a transformation of our current cultural clearing. Our technological clearing is the cause of our distress, yet if it were not given to us to encounter things and ourselves as resources, nothing would show up as anything at all, and no possibilities for action would make sense. And once we realize that we receive our technological understanding of being, we have stepped out of the technological of being, for we then see that what is most important in our lives is not subject to efficient enhancement – indeed, the drive to control everything is precisely what we do not control (1993, p. 307).

Based on the notion that people can be shaken out of an opiate daze created by their feverish and often unaccounted for use of technologies, social networks, and so on, societies have developed digital education and literacy, data and information legislation and regulation, and the very concept of the data subject. It is indeed ironic that in the last few years a trend has arisen for self-monitoring use of personal devices, notably smart phones, by downloading an app to one's phone which collects data on how and when you use the phone (Gibbs, 2018). Yet, smart phones are ubiquitous and profligate and the prime example of a mode that 'challenges' users as ones to whom data relates in this manner of resourcing, in the way an ocean ceases to be a body of deep water when challenged for reserves of oil by rigs, drills, and all the scientific prowess of modern extractive practices. This is the thinking underpinning the datus quo, which Heidegger refers to as setting upon (2011, p. 224). Clumsily, but with obvious rationale, standardised thinking of this sort leads to the commercial, and non-commercial, mantra 'data is the new oil', transforming ones to whom data relates into resources ripe for extraction like any other site in nature. Nature is up for grabs and human nature is no less valuable on this score. This despite centuries of developing protections over the integrity of the human subject and feeding, what we perhaps are only now recognising as the lethal preponderance for humanity to consider itself above all other forms of nature. 'The revealing that rules throughout modern technology has the character of setting-upon, in the sense of challenging-forth', Heidegger argues, continuing,

> Such challenging happens in that the energy concealed in nature is unlocked, what is unlocked is transformed, what is transformed is stored up, what is stored up is in turn distributed, and what is distributed is switched about ever anew. Unlocking, transforming, storing, distributing, and switching about are ways of revealing. But the revealing never simply comes to an end. Neither does it run off into the indeterminate. The revealing reveals to itself its own manifoldly interlocking paths, through regulating their course. This regulating itself is, for its part, everywhere secured. Everywhere everything is ordered to stand by, to be immediately on hand, indeed to stand there just so that it may be on call for further ordering. Whatever is ordered about in this way has its own standing. We call it the standing-reserve [*Bestand*] (2011, p. 224).

On the notion of *Bestand* we arguably reach the first of two keywords at the heart of Heidegger's questioning of technology with equal relevance to data. As the long quote above shows, in reaching the point of a standing-reserve through aspects of unlocking, transforming, storing, and so on, Heidegger brings us ever closer to a basis for the questioning of data, as the sine qua non of 'what is stored up', not only as a standard practice of the Information Age, but also as a standardising practice within neoliberal thought. Today, everything hinges on the say-so of data. What we cannot model slips through the fabric of social meaning woven by a super-abundance of data. As a result, certain things either cease to matter or to exist because they are not reducible to mathematical models or deemed errant to them. Data supply is the only thing constraining a techno-moral imagination who's revealing never ends. In its omnidirectional ordering, both forward into information and back into the one to whom data relates, data satisfies its own standing for man's variegated commercial and civic ends. These interlocking conditions through which we observe the emergent nature of data – data into information about a person – is a revealing on Heidegger's terms, where data and information have the texture of modern technology to them. But data as we know it today places stress on a key element of Heidegger's questioning concerning man's transformation into stranding-reserve. As Dalton *et al.* argue: 'Simply put, corporate data is meant to create profit, its veracity secondary to it economic value. In practice, this means that the everyday scale of data is the scale of the commodified data point and the individual person from whence its springs' (2016, p. 6). For Christian Fuchs, Marx's concepts of surplus-value and surplus labour time explain man's contemporary transformation into standing-reserve, both of which have assumed a new and more pervasive status in digital economies of the Information Age (2014; 2016).

I do not accept the validity of Heidegger's argument here, at least not on contemporary terms, because the phenomenon of personal data we see today has transformed all mankind into a standing reserve. Man is set upon to order by technology as Heidegger claims, but we gather and concentrate ourselves as data resources within the *datus quo* into ordering, although programming is perhaps the more apt a word in this context. Like a standby button on a device, mankind is pressed into action to programme and frame [*Gestell*] nature not for the benefit of mankind in or for nature, but for man as a self-sanctioning beneficiary of growth, efficiency, and profit as the products of challenging forth. This is so within neoliberalism which, as already suggested, stretches being across a three-fold datafication plain of primordial or passive data person (economically) (self)-enlightened data sovereign, and rights bearing and enforcing data subject. Technological activity may be, as Heidegger notes, only ever a response to 'the challenge of enframing' (2011, p. 227). *Gestell* is the second of the two keywords of relevance to our questioning of data. Enframing is the essence of modern technology for Heidegger, but, I argue, data is a better or perhaps more germane approximation of the essence of technology and technological activity that we have. Not in the sense that data powers or fuels technologies, systems, or networks within a neoliberal capitalist understanding of resource management, but data as that which challenges and sets upon man 'to order the actual as standing-reserve in accordance with the way it shows itself' (Heidegger, 2011, p. 226). Gavin Rae says of Heidegger's idea that, 'human being does not remain untouched by the enframing of technology; it itself becomes enframed so that humans become both a being in control of its environment and one at the mercy of the calculable, instrumental projects of others', a position which is understandably more insidious and venal given the role of data in that process of calculation (2012, p. 315).

The notion of data as enframing makes Heidegger's essay particularly relevant. Heidegger did not live in a world like ours and could not have conceived of the extent to which data is such a dominant, if not the dominant, cause of being, nor the fetishisitic power things such as smart phones, surveillance techniques, software and applications, and data itself, have over society. In his memorial address celebrating the 175th birthday of the composer Conradin Kreutzer on October 30, 1955, Heidegger commented on mankind's relationship with technology in a statement that seems somehow prescient in its account of 'devices' and naïve (with the gift of hindsight):

> For all of us, the arrangements, devices, and machinery of technology are to a greater or lesser extent indispensable. It would be foolish to attack technology blindly. It would be shortsighted to condemn it as the work of the devil. We depend on technical devices; they even challenge us to ever greater advances. But suddenly and unaware we find ourselves so firmly shackled to these technical devices that we fall into bondage to them. Still we can act otherwise. We can use technical devices, and yet with proper use also keep ourselves so free of them, that we may let go of them any time. We can use technical devices as they ought to be used, and also let them alone as something which does not affect our inner and real core. We can affirm the unavoidable use of technical devices, and also deny them the right to dominate us, and so to warp, confuse, and lay waste to our nature (1966, pp. 53–54).

As well as under-predicting the techno-social fate of mankind, and despite the lessons of Marx, Heidegger did not seem convinced that man could befall the further fate of becoming his own standing reserve, or, at least, he saw it as an extreme outcome, a 'precipitous fall' whereby what is unconcealed no longer concerns man as object, but only as standing reserve (2011, pp. 231–232). Yet, in the concept of enframing he gives us a penetrating means of questioning being in data, one which enables us to listen and not only obey what data or the systems that rely on it profess to be our destiny, in a way that surpasses the naivety of his age (2011, p. 230).

Notes

1. Leibniz, for example, distinguishes between truths of reason as necessary, meaning 'the reason for it can be found by analysis, that is, by resolving it into simpler ideas and truths until the primary ones are reached', and truths of fact as contingent (Leibniz, 1973, p. 184).
2. Christian Fuchs refers to prosumption within capitalism 'used for outsourcing work to users and consumers who work without or for low payment' (2016, p. 97).
3. Arthur Davidson may have been literal in his example of a computer picture but I interpret it as a metaphor for data gathered and aggregated into an individual profile or record ('picture') containing a range of information, such as age, height, weight, hair colour, eye colour, whether I have beard, and so on. That is, many of the essential characteristics that enable an impression of my appearance to be represented, yet say little or nothing about my values, beliefs, and so on. The 'picture' analogy on these terms is clearly a basic one but explains how and why the sophistication of data gathering is scaled: to constantly refine and improve the 'picture'.
4. See, for example, www.lotame.com (accessed 5 June 2020).

References

The Economist. 2010. *Data, Data Everywhere: A Special Report on Managing Information*. 27 February, pp. 3–5.

Trending Now: The Web 2.0 Data Monetization Opportunity. McKinsey & Company. https://www.mckinsey.com/client_service/telecommunications/latest_thinking/~/media/595B32BE570D4759BA4F1D7ADDAF81A1.ashx (accessed 5 June 2020).

Bastani, Aaron. 2019. *Fully Automated Luxury Communism: A Manifesto*. London: Verso.

Baudrillard, Jean. 1996. *The System of Objects*. Translated by James Benedict. London: Verso.

Bogost, Ian. 2012. *Alien Phenomenology, or What It's Like to Be a Thing*. Minneapolis: University of Minnesota Press.

Bosteels, Bruno. 2014. *The Actuality of Communism*. London: Verso.

Caputo, John D. 2018. *Hermeneutics: Facts and Interpretation in the Age of Information*. London: Penguin.

Carman, Taylor. 2007. Authenticity. In *A Companion to Heidegger*. Hubert L. Dreyfus and Mark A. Wrathall. Hoboken, NJ: John Wiley & Sons, pp. 285–296.

Couldry, Nick and Andreas Hepp. 2017. *The Mediated Construction of Reality*. Cambridge: Polity.

Dalton, Craig M., Linnet Taylor and Jim Thatcher. 2016. Critical Data Studies: A Dialog on Data and Space. *Big Data & Society*. Vol. 3, No. 1, pp. 1–9.

Dreyfus, Hubert L. 1993. Heidegger on the Connection Between Nihilism, Art, Technology, and Politics. *The Cambridge Companion to Heidegger*. Edited by Charles B. Guignon. Cambridge: Cambridge University Press, pp. 289–316.

Floridi, Luciano. 2013. *The Ethics of Information*. Oxford: Oxford University Press.

Fuchs, Christian. 2014. *Digital Labour and Karl Marx*. Abingdon: Routledge.

Fuchs, Christian. 2016. *Reading Marx in the Information Age*. Abingdon: Routledge.

Gibbs, Samuel. 2018. I Tracked My iPhone Usage for a Week and This Is What I Learned. *The Guardian*, 12 July. https://www.theguardian.com/technology/2018/jul/12/i-tracked-my-iphone-usage-for-a-week-and-this-is-what-i-learned (accessed 12 June 2020).

Heidegger, Martin. 1966. *Discourse on Thinking*. Translated by John M. Anderson and E. Hans Freund. New York: Harper Perennial.

Heidegger, Martin. 1996. *Being and Time*. Translated by Joan Stambaugh. Albany: State University of New York Press.

Heidegger, Martin. 2011. *Basic Writings*. Edited by David Farrell Krell. Abingdon: Routledge.

Herian, Robert. 2020. Blockchain, GDPR, and Fantasies of Data Sovereignty. *Law, Innovation and Technology*. Vol. 12, No. 1, pp. 156–174.

Hoy, Meredith. 2018. Modern Science, Nature and the Phenomenology of Data Collection. *Leonardo*. Vol. 51, No. 3, pp. 302–303.

Iliadis, Andrew and Federica Russo. 2016. Critical Data Studies: An Introduction. *Big Data & Society*. Vol. 3, No. 1, pp. 1–7.

Leibniz, Gottfried Wilhelm. 1973. *Philosophical Writings*. Edited by G. H. R. Parkinson. London: J.M. Dent & Sons.

Lyon, David. 2019. Surveillance Capitalism, Surveillance Culture and Data Politics. *Data Politics: Worlds, Subjects, Rights*. Edited by Dider Bigo, Engin Isin, and Evelyn Ruppert. Abingdon: Routledge, pp. 64–78.

Mirowski, Philip. 2014. *Never Let a Serious Crisis Go To Waste*. London: Verso.

Morton, Timothy. 2018. *Being Ecological*. London: Penguin.

Pasquale, Frank. 2015. *The Black Box Society: The Secret Algorithms That Control Money and Information*. Cambridge: Harvard University Press.

Powers, Richard. 2018. *The Overstory*. London: Vintage.

Posner, Eric A. and E. Glen Weyl. 2018. Want Our Personal Data? Pay for It. *The Wall Street Journal*, 20 April. https://www.wsj.com/articles/want-our-personal-data-pay-for-it-1524237577 (accessed 19 May 2020).

Rae, Gavin. 2012. Being and Technology: Heidegger on the Overcoming of Metaphysics. *Journal of the British Society of Phenomenology*. Vol. 43, No. 3, pp. 305–325.

Rockmore, Tom. 1992. *On Heidegger's Nazism and Philosophy*. Berkeley: University of California Press.

Simanowski, Roberto. 2016. *Data Love: The Seduction and Betrayal of Digital Technologies*. New York: Columbia University Press.

Wolin Richard. (ed.). 1998. *The Heidegger Controversy: A Critical Reader*. Cambridge: The MIT Press.

Žižek, Slavoj. 2009. *First and Tragedy, Then as Farce*. London: Verso.

4   Data with subject

Introduction

Chapters 1 and 2 presented a survey of the *datus* quo, whilst Chapter 3 offered a countervailing theoretical discussion on being in data aimed to provoke distinct ways of thinking about the conventional expectations and perceptions of data subjectivity and personal data that inform the *datus quo.* Here we continue our critique by considering personal data and the data subject as independent yet interdependent ontological objects in ways that reflect on and develop the work of Heidegger. To give these notions some context I will consider how we might further transform conventional expectations and perceptions of personal data and the data subject through narratives that re-imagine data being other to the legal legitimisation of exploitative economic, data-reliant business models that we find at the heart of the *datus quo.* Chiefly this means re-evaluating the proximities and tensions within relationships between subjects and (personal) data by expanding on the overproduction of being that metaphors such as 'shedding' and 'leaching' represent.

Examples discussed during this chapter will be familiar, while others will be less so, pushing at the limit of our thinking about data and data subjectivity as phenomena. The examples I will explore include data as waste; data desire lines, re-evaluations of business efficiency and efficacy built on informal and ad hoc data practices; and, last, data 'tonsure' – a reference to the ritual, ecstatic, and sacrificial practice involving the shaving of the scalp of devotees I suggest here to focus on a peculiar but germane combination of ritualistic, cosmetic, and commodified interpretations of personal data and data subjectivity. With descriptive data narratives such as these, and with the aid of the theoretical position known as object-orientated ontology (OOO), this chapter will explore a breadth of phenomenal notions of personal data and the data subject as objects with being independent of and interdependent on one another.

The object to whom the object relates

Central to my thinking here is a speculation on the ontological separation of data and subject. I do not mean this as a Cartesian object/ subject dichotomy. Instead, data and subject as two objects that withdraw from, relate to one another, yet never attain a unity of function or purpose that allows anyone (controller, observers, data analysts, etc.) to point with absolute clarity and certainty at the 'one to whom data relates' as a knowable entity. Like the decision in the Irish Court of Appeal, *Nowak v DPC* [2020] IECA 174, which decided that data subjects could have a 'copy' of their data in an 'intelligible form' but not the 'original' data itself under a subject access request, data and subject never come together, they only exist in analogue (as copies and references). With this ontological position in mind, I want to test existing ideas and provoke fresh thinking about personal data and the data subject on two main fronts: legally and culturally. For example, fresh thinking confronting the unclear legal status of bodily material where personal data falls within definitions of bodily material deemed valuable and 'retained, stored, and used for a wide range of purposes', but subject to the 'no property rule' (Wall, 2015, p. 2). And fresh thinking going beyond related cultural statements, such as the following by Luciano Floridi, which act as an excellent starting point for our discussion but not a conclusion:

> If personal information is finally acknowledged to be a constitutive part of someone's personal identity and individuality, then one day it may become strictly illegal to trade in some of personal information, exactly as it is illegal to trade in human organs (including one's own) or slaves. At the same time, one might relax one's attitude towards some kinds of 'dead personal information' that, like 'dead pieces of oneself', are not really or no longer constitutive of oneself. One should not sell one's kidney, but can certainly sell one's hair or be rewarded for giving blood. We are constantly leaving behind a trail of personal data, pretty much in the same sense in which we are shedding a huge trail of dead cells. The fact that nowadays digital ICTs allow our data trails to be recorded, monitored, processed, and used for social, political, or commercial purposes is a strong reminder of our informational nature as individuals and might be seen as a new level

of ecologism, as an increase in what is recycled and a decrease in what is wasted (2013, p. 245).

One of the fundamental shifts I want to explore here deals with rejecting the dead-ness of personal information that Floridi mentions and which infuses legal interpretations of property as things other than living bodily material. Following the work of Heidegger in particular, I am interested in considering a *continuation of things* outside the frame of human interest, right, or intervention. Hence, the two objects, personal data and data subject, for me possess a fundamental parity that speaks to but does not end in the notion of a 'data object' as an interpretive expression of a particular data set determined by human ingenuity or reason, or that 'who we are in terms of data depends on how our data is spoken for' (Cheney-Lippold, 2019, pp. 47–48). Moreover, I am interested in data as a pre-algorithmic object and thus echo Niklaus Wirth's 'intuitive feeling that data precede algorithms' (quoted in Bucher, 2018, p. 22). Instead, we mis-align with 'our data' and it mis-aligns with us, which leads, more often than not, to unfortunate conclusions of 'dead information' that no longer appears to relate or belong to, legally or otherwise, a subject.

Akin to Jesse Wall's concern regarding the ambiguity of the legal status of bodily material separated from *its* body, the question here is whether, and to what extent, we ought to respect or even consider personal data as material separate from the body (data subject) in question, and as extension or recalibration of the Kantian tradition, through Heidegger, which insists data is all we have because things always withdraw from and elude us (Wall, 2015, p. 3). Unlike Wall, however, I do not view as lifeless or lacking vitality the object nature that they assume bodily material to have – for OOO that is an example of an anthropocentrism that denies non-human material and things being. I agree that where this object thinking is problematic concerns law's dealing with such material through mechanisms of use and possession as it would any other material, including, I would add, raw materials and commodities such as those identified throughout this book in terms of the *datus quo* ('data is the new oil').

As I stated in the previous chapter, in a radical sense this viewpoint aims to push past what Timothy Morton calls the 'transcendental gap' between a thing and how it appears, its data (2018, p. 22). We ought not to think of data only as 'thing-data' – data indistinguishable from its thing, such as personal data from its subject – but as distinguishable objects that miss the mark of the person to whom they are personal. Hence, personal data with subject. This conjures up dislocation rather than relation. A misbehaving shadow as an object that defies its 'owner', such as we find in the work of Chinese designer Weng Xinyu (翁昕煜) for example. In Weng's project, 'Good Medicine Tastes Bitter (良药苦)', the designer created several everyday objects that challenge design conventions by asking two fundamental questions: do products always have to satisfy the users; and how can products intentionally made not to be useful affect our perception and under-standing of them?[1] The project included the 'Angry Lamp' that turns itself off if it believes humans are wasting energy; 'Tangible Memory', a photo frame that slowly blurs the photo it holds if left untouched for a period; and 'Time Killer', a clock that kills itself by cutting through its own body if nobody is present to look at it.[2] Weng's designs imitate the autonomy I propose for data separated from a subject. Although, as we will see, the step further beyond the notion of a misbehaving shadow or Weng's un-useful objects is to remove the need for human involvement or intervention for things or objects to have meaning.

The work of three authors for whom Heidegger's notion of being offers an important starting point, but is not the place where the story of being in the world ends, provides the backdrop to this section. Falling at different points within a field of theoretical inquiry known as OOO, Jane Bennett, Timothy Morton, Ian Bogost, and Graham Harman each offer interesting, often subtle, yet powerful variations on materialist and immaterialist thinking and understandings of the world in which humanity finds itself as one object among many. For each, human per-ceptions and interpretations of the world are not a sole locus of being but only one among all things that exist in nature. Beginning with a *flat ontology*, therefore, the positions presented by Bennet, Bogost, and Harman insist that all things possess being independent of humanity's experience, perception, or use of them. Ian Bogost, for example, whose work remains 'flat' compared with Harman, describes flat ontology as '*all things equally exist, yet they do not exist equally.* The funeral pyre is not the same as the aardvark; the porceletta shell is not equivalent to the rugby ball. Not only is neither pair reducible to human encounter, but also neither is reducible to the other' (2012, p. 11). All things do, to follow Bennet, form part of a 'speculative onto-story', a story that highlights 'the extent to which human being and thinghood overlap, the extent to which the us and the it slip-slide into each other' (2010, pp. 3–4). As a starting point for reconsidering the relationship as data with subject, we can see that both objects are transformed by imposing a theory that insists on a fundamental schism between humanity as objects not subjects and how we relate to the data we call personal, but which is independent to us.

The context of data and subject is at once good for interrogating the premise of this theory, as the extent to which humanity 'overlaps' with and 'slip-slides' into personal data is clear. But it is very much complicated by the proposition that data is its own material object, something that seems incongruous to data only as a sensory sign or record of something else and, therefore, not its own being in the world. The legacy of Heidegger's work is obvious, and we discussed being in data as something separate from its subject in the previous chapter. The conclusion drawn from Heidegger's question of technology takes us to data as enframing of being. This means a separate phenomenological understanding of personal data, but only if it is to humans that data relates and owes its existence. OOO opens up discussions on personal data independent of what we would consider crucial to its place in the world, the one to whom the date relates. This is because OOO, and close compatriot thinking, reject the pre-eminence of human thought and experience. Instead it invites us, as human beings in the world (following Heidegger), to appreciate what we can call for convenience' sake, intersubjective being between things or objects that has nothing to do with human knowledge or understanding. As Timothy Morton explains, OOO 'doesn't make thinking, in particular, human thinking, into a special kind of access mode that truly gets at what a thing is. OOO tries to let go of anthropocentrism, which holds that humans are the centre of meaning and power' (2018, p. 34).

Letting go of things

Jane Bennett provides two important arguments, the first concerns the force exerted by thingly-power as 'vivid entities not entirely reducible to the contexts in which (human) subjects set them', and the second concerns the agency of things that 'always depends on the collaboration, cooperation, or interactive interference of many bodies and forces' (2010, p. 5 and p. 21). The latter of these two will become important in the next and final chapter of this book, but I begin with Bennett's account of things as exceeding humanity's perception of or interest in them, or as Bennett puts it, things 'in excess of their association with human meanings, habits, or projects' (2010, p. 4). Key to understanding how things exist in such a way is to consider the life of waste or debris. This 'afterlife' of things, discarded or used-up by humanity, is for Bennett a sign not of where the being of things ends but where it arguably becomes most prominent and its vitality begins. Things that humanity no longer has a use for or sensory interest in (to see, hear, smell, or touch, etc.) do not make them cease to exist in the world. Instead, they continue as their own particular and peculiar manifestation of non-organic life and being. Human-made categorisations distinguish between things once considered within human perception to be what we might call 'useful', and those things that don't – what we routinely call 'waste', 'junk', or 'refuse' – as a source of meaning and reality. But it is not reality as such. It is quite the opposite in fact, because what categorisation achieves is predicated solely on a guarantee of human perceptive authority and power granted to humanity by itself. Hence, for Bennett 'a vital materiality can never really be thrown "away", for it continues its activities even as a discarded or unwarranted commodity' (2010, p. 6).

The human conclusion as to, and categorisation of, waste (debris, trash, litter, etc.) is important to Bennett's exposition of things as 'vibratory – at one moment disclosing themselves as dead stuff and at the next as live presence: junk, then claimant; inert matter, then live wire' (2010, p. 5). And, I suggest, offers us a way to frame an understanding not only of human data production(s), but also of the systematic and systemic ways in which such production is conceptualised and actualised. If we take the analogy of data's raw materiality seriously, for example, that is, ways in which economic models that mimic combustion engines that require fuel (e.g. oil) to both lubricate and power them frame data in this way, then what is useable and what is waste product features predominately in data processing and decision-making. We make a choice to exclude data as much as to include it within the economic models and other data analytical processes that bear heavily on the daily function of societies. Not only Human hands and ingenuity make these choices but also, importantly, algorithms and machine-to-machine increasingly make choices and start processes invisible to human operators.

There have to be levels of refinement prior to introducing the fuel to the engine, so to speak, but the engine itself acts as a further filtering mechanism providing processing and refinement. The data subject as a productive engine of valuable data is one way in which we can view this. Fuel combusts in the engine, generating exhaust as a waste or by-product of the combustion process. We can think of the combustible by-product as pollution, or as an opportunity for stakeholders in data and information value systems, networks, and markets to realise more stages of value from the original 'raw material'. Extraction and refinement processes are commonplace in today's world, notably not only with oil but also with water, including the treatment of sewage not only to mitigate toxins but also as a recoverable source of valuable matter. And in the time of Covid-19, recovering value from wastewater and sewage involves tracking the virus through waste systems.[3] Value, in this context, is in tracking the contents of 'waste' data conveyed by and in expelled and forgotten ('flushed') matter. The fluidity of these materials – oil, water, data – allows circulation in, around, and through human-designed systems of operation, and extraction of energy, force, and usefulness until the material is exhausted physically (e.g. no longer able to generate energy), exhausted economically (e.g. no longer able to generate value, including value based on cost-benefit analyses), or both. We can see the treatment of personal data in the same way, and not only by analogy. In reality the refinement and processing of oil, water, and data differ little when we take into consideration the minor leap of human ingenuity and imagination that insists and operates because of the scarcity value of each. This is classical property theory couched in the mores of contemporary political economy in which data exhaust or 'smog' is not a pollutant *per se*, but an opportunity for further value extraction within a concept that owners have a right to use, abuse, and alienate things. And raising the spectre of property rights, including a right of exclusion from one's property, returns us to the privacy issues and debates I touched on in earlier chapters. Hence, we find John Cheney-Lippold discussing the role privacy ought to play in defending 'a breathing space to be' from the likes of Facebook's business model that profit from commodification of data smog (2019, p. 245).

A struggle remains to understand the demotion of human authority in making judgements about what is or is not 'useful' or possessing of a particular vital materiality, as Bennett frames it. Here we stumble upon the morality of mankind's relative authority over things, between human subjects, and at its most extreme, over nature itself. It is a return to what Heidegger called the 'will to mastery', whereby 'everything depends on our manipulating technology in the proper manner as a means' and 'becomes all the more urgent the more technology threatens to slip from human control' (2011, p. 218). But it is not merely technology slipping from humanity's grasp that terrifies us and drives the will to mastery, it is losing control or rather discovering we never had control over all things in the world with which we co-exist. It is imperative, therefore, for humanity to reaffirm a hierarchy of being that places all other things in the world below it. Bennett proposes that we should see this problem from a different angle, although one that is arguably more relevant to personal data and the data subject because it focuses on responses to a general sense that 'a strong distinction between subjects and objects is needed to prevent the instrumentalization of humans' (2010, pp. 11–12). Whilst echoing the Kantian imperative that humanity ought not to be an end-in-itself, Bennett seeks to push past the force of the imperative to collapse all options not in total harmony with it by suggesting 'healthy and enabling instrumentalizations' that 'face up to the compound nature of the human self' (2010, p. 12).

It is on this point that Bennett offers a glimpse not only of a post-Kantian view of object subject relations that describe distinct ways to consider relations between data and subject, but also of a post-Heideggerian view. One in which the ultimate authority of human perception that Heidegger could not quite relinquish, despite the fundamental importance of his notion that objects withdraw from one another, encased as they are in their own being, breaks down in favour of thing-power and vital materialism. Bennett's example of the struggle to see past Kant's imperative to accept the object-status of humanity as compounded bits of matter, rather than as inviolate, coherent, and rational subjects is perhaps the best description of the one to whom data relates. 'Each human is a heterogenous compound of wonderfully vibrant, dangerously vibrant, matter', Bennett maintains, continuing,

> If matter itself is lively, then not only is the difference between subjects and objects minimized, but the status of the shared materiality of all things is elevated. All bodies become more than mere objects, as the thing-powers of resistance and protean agency are brought into sharper relief. Vital materialism would thus set up a kind of safety net for those humans who are now, in a world where Kantian morality is the standard, routinely made to suffer because they do not conform to a particular (Euro-American, bourgeois, theocentric, or other) model of personhood. The ethical aim becomes to distribute value more generously, to bodies as such. Such a newfound attentiveness to matter and its powers will not solve the problem of human exploitation or oppression, but it can inspire a greater sense of the extent to which all bodies are kin in the sense of [being] inextricably enmeshed in a dense network of relations. And in a knotted world of vibrant matter, to harm one section of the web may very well be to harm oneself (2010, p. 13).

Interpreting Bennett's position regarding personal data and data subjectivity raises questions of whether we should think of personal data only as machine-readable and calculable indicium that map or reflect momentary characteristics of a particular object or body. For example, my smart phone showing through the data it produces, collects, and transmits relative to the fact that I'm walking through a city at a particular time of day, in certain weather, past particular shops, and so on. Or whether 'data' is matter in the same way as, for example, gastrointestinal microbiota, and therefore the human object is best thought of as a community of matter built of many interacting things with diverse powers of existence. On this point of interrelated acting objects, Bennett highlights the work of Bruno Latour, namely Actor Network Theory (ANT), a position not supported at length by other adherents and contributors to the field of OOO, most notably Graham Harman, whose work, as we will see shortly, also involves important differentiations between real and sensual objects and qualities that further challenge relations between data and subject.

Important to Bennett's notion of agency, the second aspect of her work I would like to discuss, is that we take it seriously as 'congregational' rather than atomistic, and these relations between objects are key to Bennett's understanding of vital materialism (2010, p. 20). 'While the smallest or simplest body or bit may indeed express a vital impetus, conatus or *clinamen*, an actant never really acts alone', explains Bennett, instead its 'efficacy and agency always depends on the collaboration, cooperation, or interactive interference of many bodies and forces' (2010, p. 21). There is no sign that Bennett's reference to 'bits' is anything other than a colloquial description of smaller pieces in a larger whole, but the linguistic link to data makes it impossible not to seize on her choice of terminology for present purposes. So, if we read 'bit' as 'data' it presents a useful and more detailed description of data as matter making up a larger body, rather than as a mere indicator of the characteristics of the body to whom it relates, or as indications of other bits making up the body. What I am proposing, therefore, is that, as data are 'leached' or 'shed' – as an animal might excrete gut flora, for example – they continue not only to exist for sensory collection or as raw materials to be challenged (to use Heidegger's term) for commodification, but also as commensal transmissions possessing agency. Data surround and work through humanity and other objects as a part of the 'knotted world of vibrant matter' and are not just convenient ways for humanity to measure or calculate the world – something which places into doubt that 'data' can be anything other than an empty signifier or linguistic placeholder for matter existing beyond the capabilities of human perception. In a break from Heidegger's humanist conceit, this is a view of data divorced from human purpose, neither ready-to- or present-at-hand solely for the benefit of mankind. 'We are not used to reading stories without human heroes', claims Anna Lowenhaupt Tsing, and 'allowing only human protagonists into our stories is not just ordinary human bias; it is a cultural agenda tied to dreams of progress through modernization' (2015, p. 155).

Bennett reinforces her viewpoint of the vitalism of this compounded matter further by drawing upon Deleuze's notion of assemblages as 'living, throbbing confederations that are able to function despite the persistent presence of energies that confound them from within' (2010, pp. 23–24). For me, an interest and excitement in rethinking data lies in an autonomy which excuses, alludes, or exceeds human need, demand, desire. Data without need of a subject, and that is, perhaps, utterly without purpose where it cannot register either in human perception or via the tools and technologies built to extend the reach of human perception. Importantly the *datus quo* ceases to be an accurate portrayal of data given by subjects for a particular set of purposes, but a well-engineered fantasy of control in which humanity has final say over the purposes of data, including commercial markets as the only means to undercover or unleash the true power of data. What humanity has no use for it cannot, does, or will not see. There are several elements to that statement that require brief clarification. Use, for example, means little today I suggest outside of economic value, including the fundamental notion of *usufruct* as a right to enjoy the property of another without destroying it. Personal data relating to 'me', 'you', 'them', or 'us' must, therefore, drive an economic engine to be worthy of consideration by 'me', 'you', 'them', or 'us'. What humanity sees in data is a matter of engineered collation and organisation, of bureaucracy-at-large, aimed at shaping and making indicium and datum more palatable or visually appealing.

Data scientists and analysts provide insights to businesses to weed-out under-performing employees and improve efficiency, for example, but 'data' visualisations are always already inclusive of certain trends in data presentation and exclude data that militates against the convenience of pattern recognition. 'As with capitalism', Tsing argues, 'it is useful to consider science a translation machine' and this is perhaps most obvious in data science where a phalanx of technicians 'stands ready to chop off excess parts and to hammer those that remain into their proper places' (2015, p. 217). Recently pattern creation and recognition has colonised human expectations of knowledge through information industries whose feedback loops extend ever further into social, cultural, economic, and political life. But there is not necessarily a human choice of whether to consider certain data. Data will register on extra-sensory devices – for example, a weather station log might show it was 30 degrees centigrade, with 80% humidity, at 4 pm on Tuesday in my garden – without a human eye cast over it or any human perception made aware. Those precise conditions, 30 degrees centigrade, etc., are a congregation of vibrant material that lie behind the weather station 'data' reading and making it necessary to metabolise a particular lactic acid bacterium, for instance, but would not be important, therefore, because no human registered it, included or excluded the data from a particular set of insights. This is a key problem of and with the *datus quo*: it is a venal ecology in which things must concern or benefit humanity not only to be important, but to register at all.

Expectations

A position we might take based on Bennett's work is that all data exist independent of the objects that produce or generate them. Although, Bennett never ventures upon a discussion of objects that are expressly data-like, she provides an interesting case-study of the failure of the electrical grid in North America in August 2003 upon which we can map different object proliferations, movements, responsibilities, and behaviours akin to networks and systems populated by data and through which data move. In the conclusion of this case-study Bennett mentions an interesting statement made by one of the power companies involved in dealing with the 2003 blackout, which includes reference to so-called loop flows, 'which occur when power takes a route form producer to buyer different from the intended path' (2010, p. 28). As vital materials, the electrons that make up what we ordinarily call 'power' appear to attain autonomy by moving through the grid in a manner that confounds human expectation. The claim being made is not one of electron sentience or conscious choice, but an independence and separation from the human will to mastery. Another way to understand this is as a mode of informality operating against the formality of the 'intended path' *qua* electricity grid, what I call a *desire line*. You will probably use a desire line in your life or already rely on one to make a habitual journey on foot or bicycle just that bit quicker. At the very least you will have seen such lines criss-crossing the grass of a local park between 'formal' pathways or bisecting a verge by the side of a major road to give the user a more direct route to the other side. We can understand a desire line, therefore, as an informal path that enables direct journeys, what we might also call short-cuts or in some circumstances a detour. As well-trodden pathways, desire lines imply a wish for and will to straightforwardness and greater efficiency than planned spaces can provide.

This is not the place to discuss the broader characteristics of desire lines in depth. But desire lines offer ways of understanding variability of movement through, what are more often than not, predetermined and defined spaces. Hence, when Bennett talks of 'loop flows' these refer to electrons not free to go where they please but only to enjoy movement *within* the electricity grid, in directions that are unpredictable and confounding to human expectations of their movement. Similarly, a conventional impression of a desire line is as a pathway cutting through parks and other civic spaces. And these paths show human or animal movement *within* the boundaries of a particular and defined space. They show a constant and often productive tension between formality and informality within networks and systems. With both examples above, we know that the predetermined spaces (networks, grids, or systems) can only contain a partial impression of the movement and behaviour of things. There is more vitality occurring beyond the boundaries that we cannot see and do not understand. If the informality caught within the system is a threat to the human will to mastery, what occurs outside of the limit increases that threat. In terms of data, we know that data are manipulated to create certain impressions and favour particular actionable insights. The income stream of data in these cases might not be predictable but is expected in some form, what we might otherwise refer to as 'data behaving badly'. The task is simply to discipline the data and make it do what we require of it – put it on a formal pathway. But like objects in any predetermined formal spaces in which informality breeds, data is an object that exceeds what we know or expect of it. It both behaves informally and beyond any sensory capacity of knowing it at all.

The analytic capabilities and capacities of OOO may not even be a prominent feature of its phenomenological largesse, one that allows us to consider data (its *phenomena,* materiality, purpose, value, etc.) from alternative points of view, including that there is no reasonable human point of view of data at all; no access to the *noumena* of the thing-in-itself – to use Kantian terms. Graham Harman, OOOs major advocate, considers aesthetics key to working through this philosophical conundrum posed by Kant and thus OOO as a position for theorising all things turns to aesthetics, art, and metaphor and a means of allowing objects to speak. Likewise, Ian Bogost sees metaphor as a means of speculating about the 'inner life' of what he prefers to call 'units' rather than objects (2012, p. 61). As Harman explains, 'once we move outside ethics, it becomes immediately clear that all objects have a noumenal side as well. We do not have direct access to plastic-bags-in-themselves any more than we do to human-beings-in-themselves; in both cases we only encounter these things phenomenally, not noumenally' (2018, p. 69). The indirectness of relations between objects (or the impossibility of direct relations) brings Harman to a conclusion of five features of metaphor, including that metaphor 'does not try to give us thoughts or perceptions about an object, since these would merely give us an external view of the thing in question' (2018, p. 86). Further, Harman emphasises the importance of metaphor by building on Husserl's distinction between real and sensual qualities and objects, proposing that metaphor involves the withdrawal of a real object from its sensual qualities, replaced instead by 'the only RO [real object] that is not withdrawn from the situation: I myself, a real experiencer of the metaphor' (2018, p. 84).

Meanwhile Bogost, following Harman's lead, proposes an opportunity to deploy metaphor to 'grasp alien objects' perceptions of one another', a suggestion that places any object in the place of the real experiencer of the metaphor (2012, p. 67). Where Harman and Bogost's exposition on the function of metaphor in mediating relations between separate objects, such as data and subject, becomes relevant in the present discussion is Bogost's example of photography to sense the world, and thus, in Kantian terms, of sensing data about a world of things we have no access to.[4] In the previous chapter we used the metaphor (some may argue an analogy) of a 'picture' to describe how an emergence of data collection and data banks altered how we are represented and seen by people, businesses, institutions, and government in the last fifty years of the Information Age. A picture, like data manipulated to achieve a particular result, tells a story and establishes certain expectations. One only has to think of the importance photography has assumed in the Information Age for selling goods, promoting ideas, and so on, to recognise the power of images to build and destroy trust and social capital. For Arthur Davidson, the Labour Member of Parliament for Accrington speaking in the debate on the Control of Personal Information Bill in 1972, this amounted to depersonalisation whereby, 'instead of the computer picture being like me, I tend to become like the computer picture' (Hansard HC Deb. vol. 835 col. 1004, 21 April 1972). In Bogost's example of photography we move from depersonalisation to a picture that is alien; other terms but, I suggest, both speak to the same fundamental misalignment between personal data and data subject. The sensor on a camera captures light reflected by an object and enables the camera to 'see', yet no two cameras see in the same way and, importantly, interpreting the picture by the human eye renders the object in the picture more alien still. And this latter point returns us to the anthropocentrism of the metaphorical enterprise and cannot resolve the expectation that humanity has of its eminent domain over a world of things. As Bogost highlights, 'we form these theories, we mount accounts of why and how humans ought to behave in and towards the universe, but not about how other objects ought to behave in relation to it' (2012, p. 74).

Data tonsure

So far, I have made the case for personal data and data subjects as objects that withdraw from one another and possess being and agency rooted in humanity and non-humanity alike. But also objects that rely upon interdependency with other objects no matter if they cannot touch and concern each other as networked or commensurable objects or achieve communality at distance through a medium or third. As with Heidegger's work, the speculative realist conclusions of OOO do not resist the ideological forces of political economy underpinning and driving forward the *datus quo*. The sorts of forces defined by Marx and summed up by Tsing, when she states that, 'In capitalist logics of commodification, things are torn from their life-worlds to become objects of exchange' (2015, p. 121). Ideology is something that does not feature prominently in OOO at all, and where it has a political agenda, it would have to be the mission against anthropocentrism, and by extension the right that humanity assumes for itself to master all nature, that flat ontology promotes. OOO does, however, offer a way to disrupt the smooth flow of ideology, notably neoliberal capitalism and the illusions of individual (or non-communal) capacity manufactured within and by it, by challenging many of the taken-for-granted assumptions that provide enduring frameworks around modern societies. For example, by challenging the taken-for-granted assumption of the inertness of objects that only humanity can animate or give meaning to as private property and commodities through rights frameworks, use, abuse, alienation, licence, interests, and so on.

The parity between object and things that flat ontology promotes does not prevent notions of possession or ownership outright, but it makes us question the appropriateness and validity of such notions. This is a challenge to the classical property rights theory in which we find a requirement 'that the object is capable of introducing a state of affairs that is willed, or intended, by the individual' (Wall, 2015, p. 85). OOO seeks to puncture these assumptions and complacencies by attacking an interminable anthropocentrism, one that law, as the long shadow of man's social and political economic ingenuity, supports and maintains. To conclude this chapter, I want to offer a final example that aims to shift perceptions of data again by exploring personal data and data subject interdependency and entanglement in terms of data as hair, and especially in a ritualistic and sacrificial form that I refer to as data tonsure.

Offering hair as a rite of spiritual passage and ritual devotion is well documented internationally, associated as it is with all major world religions. As a metaphor for accessing particular bonds and entanglements between the objects personal data and data subject, data tonsure is also a starting point for re-describing and re-imagining well-documented processes of datafication and data commodification within modernity's theocratic domain *par excellence*, capitalism, as I shall describe shortly. First, however, data is present genetically in hair. And hair, in turn, is a vehicle for object data, meaning hairy data, as a predicate for data tonsure, is never only a metaphorical flourish but a two-way understanding of how subjects relate to 'their' data. The situating of data in hair is not a radical proposition. Forensic science has long relied on hair to provide evidence in criminal and more recently civil cases (e.g. family courts) precisely because humans shed hair abundantly and regularly and we record certain behaviours and environmental factors in strands of our hair as data sources (e.g. *In re H (A Child) (Care Proceedings: Hair Strand Testing)* [2017] EWFC 64).

We all, by shedding hair, intermingle with and become part of our environments at a dusty level of discarded matter. It is one way we can see being in the world. Until recently, I had long hair. I have now shaved my head (not as an act of tonsure, I must add) yet still continue to find long strands of hair sharing the environment with me, entangled in sweaters and under sofa cushions. A single hair can place us in a particular location, with certain people at a certain time, much like the location ping on a smartphone GPS – although not as efficiently or conveniently. But as Bogost reminds us, scientific explanations, such as those involved in forensics, are stuck endlessly explaining constantly withdrawing objects. Hence, he further maintains, 'Scientific discoveries have a magical flavour, offering lurid descriptions of how things "really" work. And those magical discoveries may even describe some of the effects of object interactions. But to understand how something operates on its surroundings, or they on it, is not the same as understanding how that other thing *understands* those operations' (2012, p. 63).

So, a strand of hair is 'mine' because it once grew from my head and was nourished by the processes of my body, but it's being in the world did not cease when it became detached from my head and fell silently into a new stage of being. Instead, the hair created bonds and entanglements with the object sweater – anyone who has tried to remove hair from a sweater will know how strong those bonds can be – and the object sofa that have nothing to do with me and withdraw from my understanding of them. Whilst a single hair continues to 'speak me' through information about my health and well-being stored in (what forensics would aim to pinpoint to provide evidence of drug or alcohol use, for example), additional factors effecting the material integrity of the hair are because of intermingling and entangling with other objects in new environments that reveal little about me (as an object or subject) at all. The hair's being in the world continues, and as a source of data also continues in ways that no longer only 'speak me' but reflect several other ontic entanglements.

The documentary *Good Hair* (2009) looks at entrepreneurial practices of harvesting hair, mostly from India, for markets in African American hair extensions (weaves) in the United States. As the film highlights, those taking part in the ceremonial ritual of tonsure in Indian Hindu temples, notably the Tirumala Venkateswara Temple in Southern India, do so willingly and in the belief that the shaving of the head is an important sacrifice within the ambit of Hindu scripture (Karthikeyan, 2009). But devotees are unaware that the hair is going to overseas markets, nor are they made aware how much it is worth. This is, I suggest, a wonderful example of data tonsure *qua* personal data sourcing as a point of capital exploitation. Short of claiming devotees are 'farmed' for their hair (a point the film raises), how should we understand the bonds and relationships between hair givers (donors), sellers, and consumers (wearers or users)? The hair markets in countries such as India, Malaysia, and Vietnam are regulated in terms of import and export requirements, but imperfect in terms of guarantees of quality for consumers or reasonable recompense for donors (Mitchell, 2004; Rai, 2004; Refiney29, 2018). And, as *Good Hair* portrays it, this is an industry that extracts value by literally sweeping-up the commodity before the tonsure ceremony is complete, giving donors (devotees) no bargaining power or authority. Perhaps without this enterprise in place, they would leave shaved hair to perish and rot on temple floors across India. In which case businesses in collecting the hair act as a form of waste disposal or recycling, or, rather, what might we might euphemistically call a 'circular economy' aimed at re-finding value in rubbish, unwanted, left over, or left behind things, including shaved hair.

Following our earlier discussion of Bennett's work we can say that this practice of commodifying hair based on the notion it is a waste product is a particular categorisation, one designed to deny other understandings of hair's being. A notion that has particular relevance given tonsure's importance as a spiritual rite for devotees who believe the hair goes to God as a blessing not to international markets in wigs and weaves. In place of money, precious stones, or other material artefacts of value, hair is often the only thing a devote possesses that they are able to offer to the Gods. The contrast between givers and consumers of hair for a beauty industry that trades in material generated by the faith and belief of temple devotees is even more stark in the 2008 documentary (*Hair India*, 2008). Like *Good Hair, Hair India* reveals how temple devotees, who sometimes prepare for years for the tonsure ceremony, do not understand what happens to their hair once they have shaved it. Raffaele Brunett, one of the filmmakers, maintains in a blog post for the news channel *Al Jazeera*, following the screening of the documentary on the channel's Witness programme, that the donors don't care (Hair India, 2014). 'They want to make a sacrifice to God and wouldn't take any money for that', Brunett claims, 'People are donating their hair for a spiritual reason as a sacrifice to God. For them the hair was something they got rid of and whatever may happen to it afterwards is none of their concern' (Hair India, 2014).

Even if the hair is something 'they got rid of', as Brunett argues, the shaved hair is not a waste product *per se* for a devotee because it forms part of the fulfilment of their humility, given in divine deliverance to God. It is wrong to claim devotees do not care what happens to the hair offered by them and taken from their heads because the hair's 'destination' as defined by the ritual of tonsure is of paramount importance. Hesitation and uncertainty over committing oneself to the ceremony, a theme explored throughout *Hair India*, is evidence of the seriousness with which devotees take the ceremony and all its meanings combined. For a business to trade in and profit from the products of faith and belief might appear crass but is undoubtedly a common practice rooted in the ignorance of devotees, and also, often, of the consumers of the hair products sold in markets across the United States and elsewhere.[5] As Saritha Rai maintains, 'most Indians who offer their hair in religious devotion are unaware that it is made into wigs that are sold abroad – mainly in Europe and the United States – most of those who buy the wigs are equally unaware of the religious aspect involved in the collecting of human hair for commercial use' (2004; Prendergast, 2015, p. 24). Arguably this elides the dignity with which devotees commit themselves to tonsure and, albeit to a lesser extent, the dignity of consumers may assume in wearing the wigs and weaves made from the hair.

What a comparison between hair and personal data offers to understand personal data as a giving of oneself will hopefully be clear from the example above. The comparison is not a literal one, nor is it meant to be. But, to summarise, it is important to note at least three crucial factors. First, like the international industries that have grown-up around tonsured hair, we regulate personal data markets (through the likes of General Data Protection Regulation, GDPR). But similar to markets in hair, regulating personal data collection, storage, and use by commercial actors and governments is imperfect and under constant strain from transnationalism (moving data around the world) and the ingenuity of businesses and enterprises constantly looking for new, more efficient and abundant revenue streams. The data laws and regulations discussed earlier in this book under the aegis of the *datus quo* do not prevent the exploitation of the one to whom data relates but creates a normative backdrop in which exploitation becomes a normal, invisible, and acceptable everyday feature of individuals *qua* data subjects. Like devotees, data subject's give of themselves for just about any social need. But in particular under the theocratic (or cultic[6]) spirit of capitalist consumerism, through monitored shopping habits and rampant social networking and device use, and sometimes also with a sense of civic duty and responsibility, as with census data, political polling, health and well-being statistics, or, as we will see in the final chapter, to aid in the fight against disease, including pandemic viruses such as Covid-19. Second, the exploitative practices of information industries that extract, collect, and market personal data do so reliant upon a culture of ignorance as to the 'destination', purpose, or value of extracted data. Like devotees, data subjects have their data swept away with little or no idea of what they have consented to, how the data is used or what it is worth. 'Framing is important here', argues Lizzie O'Shea – to which we might add, to echo Heidegger, *enframing* is important here – 'Companies collect data, rather than – as is often claimed – we give it away willingly', she continues,

> Both constructions of the process are technically true, in the sense that the collection of our data is impossible without formal consent, but that provides only a very limited picture of the phenomenon. Consent is in no way meaningful when online spaces are designed around the expectation that it will be given and rarely offer users an active choice in how their data will be used or managed. It is as though obtaining consent were a mere formality, secondary to another purpose (2019, p. 15).

Further, Nick Couldry and Ulises A. Mejias maintain,

> The representatives of data colonialism try to convince us that there is nothing hollow in our assent to their order, that we are choosing familiar values of connection and human solidarity when we choose this datafied social order. They tell us that we need to go on connecting with and through them. But this is a ruse. The ruse depends on inducing human beings to forget ways of living that were left behind when we came to spend so much time servicing the social quantification sector. We are, all of us, part of the ruse. The greatest threat that data colonialism poses is that, in time, it works too well for us to want to live any other kind of existence, so that our complicity in losing hold on the possibility of freedom becomes complete (2019, p. 215).

Whilst I agree with some of what Couldry and Mejias say, as this chapter has shown, our understanding of data and personal data does not and should not begin and end with humanity's sole use, abuse, and alienation of it. Third, therefore, the colonisation that Couldry and Mejias speak of within capitalism insists on a view of data with being related to the purposes of human masters. It is a statement that reaffirms the will to mastery Heidegger spoke about, whereby data gives humanity a sense of control over the environment and nature, but equally over itself as ideological adherents. As I say, I don't disagree with this view of data, and I base the first two points above on just such a view of data exploitation and commodification within neoliberal capitalism. Akin to the hair of devotees, personal data might be the only thing an individual possesses, the only thing of real, creditable value, although the extent of that value may be unclear to or hidden from them. But I am also keen to understand data differently, including as being in a world of objects we recognise via flat ontology. The other side of Couldry and Mejias' notion – that it is data colonising humanity and not humanity's venal use of data that achieves that colonisation – also raises questions of approaches that place personal data (or any data) on a level, ontic plain with humanity. Whereby we ought to take data's being as seriously as humanity's being. In fact, we could say that Couldry and Mejias are correct when they suggest (albeit not in terms of flat ontology) that it is data, not mankind, committed to colonisation. The subtitle of their book, 'how data is colonizing human life and appropriating it for capitalism' involves the further consideration that humanity is the slave of a gang master (data) and the absolute master (capitalism), a three-way tension between separate objects and separate modes of being in the world.

How do the three factors outlined above relate? On the one hand, we can say that personal data as a separate object from the data subject is precisely what capitalism thrives on. Commercial interests with algorithmic business models built on and around personal data do not want or need the messiness or inefficiencies that accompany individual people, they want simple input/output risk defiant certainties concerning population types and cohorts. To have present, therefore, a seemingly unargumentative value source in personal data, explains how data has become the chief commercial and informatic industrial raw material of the last forty years. Drilling-down deeper in greater stores of individual or personal data does not bring analytics any closer to the essence of the individual as data subject for capital exploitation, or any other purpose. The personal data as a separate object stands to show we are never aligned with what we call personal data. This data is never truly 'mine'. The argument for personal data's separate being in world disturbs assumptions of data's unfettered raw materiality. My use of OOO and reference to the ritual of tonsure anticipates complexities rather than taken-for-granted simplicities concerning personal data with data subjects but does not assume personal data will soon merit parity with human being or interests – that flat ontological utopia is not on the horizon and may not be warranted. Tonsure provides a scene in which we can see different objects playing-out within the contemporary theocratic or cultic capitalism addicted to data. And in a last flourish I offer a vision of the hairy data analogy that brings us up to date with discourse on data sovereignty, that ideal in which a data subject controls *in toto* 'their' data. And that vision is of the weave or wig itself, a metaphor for data self-care as at once a cosmetic, commodified, and devotional sacrifice bound-up in the splendour of artifice, beautification, costume, and the veritable zhooshing of the self, ready for the digital gaze.

Notes

1. http://wengxinyu.com/project/Bitter-Design/ (accessed 7 July 2020).
2. http://wengxinyu.com/project/Bitter-Design/ (accessed 7 July 2020).
3. https://www.gov.uk/government/news/group-to-measure-for-coronavirus-prevalence-in-waste-water (accessed 14 July 2020).
4. There is, of course, a neat connection in this example with Warren and Brandeis' initial outline of privacy, and its links to present-day approaches to data management, based on the intrusive nature of society press photographers in the nineteenth century.

5. This is not the place to discuss the relationship between religion and business, needless to say those who make a business from collecting hair from tonsure ceremonies in India's Hindu temples are far from the only ones exploiting the human frailty for faith, belief, and devotion to God.
6. In his essay, Capitalism as Religion, Walter Benjamin makes the claim that capitalism has clear religious structure yet 'no specific body of dogma, no theology', hence in capitalism 'things have meaning only in their relationship to the cult' (Benjamin, 1996, p. 288).

References

Good Hair. 2009. [Documentary Film]. Jeff Stilson. dir. USA: HBO Films.

Hair India. 2008. [Documentary Film]. Raffaele Brunetti, Marco Leopardi. dirs. Italy: B&B Film.

Hair India. 2014. *Al* Jazeera, 23 January. https://www.aljazeera.com/ programmes/witness/2010/01/2010127121316920743.html (accessed 18 March 2020) (accessed 23 July 2020).

The Truth About Where Hair Extensions Come From. 2018. [YouTube] Refinery29, 9 June. https://www.youtube.com/watch?v=VlZ1SWLBfPE (accessed 23 July 2020).

Benjamin, Walter. 1996. *Selected Writings*, Volume 1, 1913–1926. Edited by Marcus Bullock, Michael W. Jennings. Cambridge: Belknap Harvard.

Bennett, Jane. 2010. *Vibrant Matter: A Political Ecology of Things*. Durham: Duke University Press.

Bogost, Ian. 2012. *Alien Phenomenology, or What It's Like to Be a Thing*. Minneapolis: University of Minnesota Press.

Bucher, Taina. 2018. *If … Then: Algorithmic Power and Politics*. Oxford: Oxford University Press.

Cheney-Lippold, John. 2019. *We Are Data: Algorithms and the Making of Our Digital Selves*. New York: New York University Press.

Couldry, Nick and Ulises A. Mejias. 2019. *The Costs of Connection: How Data Is Colonizing Human Life and Appropriating It for Capitalism*. Stanford: Stanford University Press.

Floridi, Luciano. 2013. *The Ethics of Information*. Oxford: Oxford University Press.

Harman, Graham. 2018. *Object-Orientated Ontology: A New Theory of Everything*. London: Penguin.

Heidegger, Martin. 2011. *Basic Writings*. Edited by David Farrell Krell. Abingdon: Routledge.

Karthikeyan, Kaliaperumal. 2009. Tonsuring: Myths and Facts. *International Journal of Trichology*. Vol. 1, No. 1, Jan–Jun, pp. 33–34.

Mitchell, Robert. 2004. $ell: Body Wastes, Information, and Commodification. *Data Made Flesh: Embodying Information*. Edited by Robert Mitchell, Phillip Thurtle. New York: Routledge, pp. 121–136.

Morton, Timothy. 2018. *Being Ecological*. London: Penguin.

O'Shea, Lizzie. 2019. *Future Histories: What Ada Lovelace, Tom Paine, and the Paris Commune Can Teach Us About Digital Technology*. London: Verso.

Prendergast, Lara. 2015. The Roots of the Matter. *The Spectator*. Vol. 327, No. 9739, p. 24.

Rai, Saritha. 2004. A Religious Tangle Over the Hair of Pious Hindus. *New York Times*, 14 July. https://www.nytimes.com/2004/07/14/world/a-religious-tangle-over-the-hair-of-pious-hindus.html (accessed 22 July 2020).

Tsing, Anna Lowenhaupt. 2015. *The Mushroom at the End of the World: On the Possibility of Life in Capitalist Ruins*. Princeton, NJ: Princeton University Press.

Wall, Jesse. 2015. *Being and Owning: The Body, Bodily Material, and the Law*. Oxford: Oxford University Press.

5   Proximate data – a conclusion

Introduction

A few years ago, on holiday in Montenegro, I stayed in the town of
Perast on the shores of the Bay of Kotor in the country's southwest.
The awe-inspiring, steep-sided Bay links to the Adriatic and cruise
ships come and go daily, bringing surges of tourists that swell the
towns and villages along the fringes of the Bay. Next to Perast, in the
middle of the Bay, are two small islands. On one, Ostrvo Sveti Đorđe
(island of Saint George), is a twelfth-century monastery. As a key
attraction, excursions to Saint George are frequent and busy. But the
island is tiny, and tourists must snake in, out, and around one another,
both inside the monastery and in the grounds that surround it. During
my visit the public's penchant for 'selfie-sticks', the telescopic poles
that allow users to attach a smart phone for taking pictures beyond
the reach of their own arm, was well established and the international
tourist crowd were unified in their use. Smart phones on sticks joined
with people using 'conventional' cameras to record moments on the
island.

Why I recall my visit to Saint George is because of the matter of
proximity. Us, the temporary islands dwellers, and the island's dimin-
utive size meant that we would inevitably appear in multiple pho-
tographs taken by people we did not know, would never know, and
would likely never meet again. Several cameras conceivably captured
me from different angles as I sat enjoying the sunshine on the island,
yet these viewpoints would never form a complete picture, only frag-
ments where there would always be one angle missing. Not only would
the picture not materialise because the various photographers were
unlikely to organise themselves to undertake piecing together their
individual shots, but also because a coherent object called 'me' captured in a composite of multiple images (*qua* data points), would never

appear but would always withdraw. Each image recorded a location (and time) with the object 'me' in it, one presence in an ontographic account involving different (en-)framed photographed objects. The 'me' was, to recall Gavin Rae from Chapter 3, 'at the mercy of the calculable, instrumental projects of others', even as those projects were merely standard tourist behaviours of taking 'selfies' and pictures of other assorted objects (2012, p. 315).

My experience on Saint George was not the first time I had considered what it means to appear randomly in someone's holiday photos. We have all undoubtedly appeared in countless of photos in this way, and latterly, and unwillingly, been 'part of someone else's reconstruction' when they share those with others in the days, weeks, months, perhaps even years afterwards (Bell, 2020, p. 18). Today we are likely to have our image taken without our consent because we just happened to be (being) in the frame, in the background forming part of the mise en scène of another's selfie, with the image stored digitally on the hard drive or in the cloud of someone we cannot know. It is highly likely that image may also be shared, again without our consent, on social media. Constrained, albeit voluntarily, on Saint George with hundreds of cameras pointing and shooting in every direction, meant a greater likelihood of being captured, caught, and written into (to evoke the Greek etymology of '-graphy') someone else's holiday memories. Why is this relevant here? There are questions of privacy raised by such situations, precisely the privacy Warren and Brandeis had in mind, in fact, as discussed in earlier chapters. But an urgent need to protect one's privacy is unlikely to lead a person to a tourist hotspot or into a jostling throng. The anonymity of the crowd is perhaps a contrary factor, one running parallel with individual concerns for privacy. Like Edgar Allan Poe's 'Man in the Crowd', we might enjoy hiding in crowds, dissolving into masses, at once a categorisable object with detail and an object of no significance at all.

> At first my observations took an abstract and generalizing turn. I looked at the passengers in masses, and thought of them in their aggregate relations. Soon, however, I descended to details, and regarded with minute interest the innumerable varieties of figure, dress, air, gait, visage, and expression of countenance.
>
> (Poe, 1998, p. 85)

Data never exists in a vacuum but intermingle and entangle like the crowds in Poe's tale, building both abstract and detailed information profiles alike that aim to reveal something of the essence of certain target communities, consumers, and cohorts. As contrapuntal processes, data cleaning fills in gaps in datasets to bring a 'picture' into focus, while 'noise' corrupts the meaning of data, renders problematic an interpretation by analysts, or is added by data managers and controllers to disguise and obscure intimate details and patterns in stored information. Hence, when we compose information as knowledge – 'analytical insights' – it comprises a litany of data objects both willing and unwilling, intentional and accidental. During this final chapter I want to talk about the increasing importance governments and societies are placing on data in the time of Covid-19, and in particular the role data is playing in providing snapshots ('pictures') of the virus' movement through national and international populations, and how data works simultaneously at abstract, generalising, and detailed levels of analysis. As the book's conclusion, this chapter will draw on some themes discussed in earlier chapters and consider them in terms of the power of data as a pandemic response.

Something happening here

Countries around the world have confronted the spread of Covid-19 by confining entire populations to their homes in mass 'lockdowns' for weeks and months. The aim was brutally simple: to stop humanity's social interaction and thus slow down and, hopefully, prevent transmission of the virus. Almost overnight humanity went from physical, tactile, jostling multitudes to atomised, home-based units, and 'social distancing' entered the global lexicon with force. Since early 2020 the planet has been more silent, had less 'seismic noise', and seen improvements, marginally, in environmental quality because of lockdown (Gibney, 2020; He *et al.*, 2020). Meanwhile, vigorous data use and production by individuals has continued because of an increase in smart phone and internet usage, messaging and streaming services, surges in video conferencing, gaming, and so on (Jackson, 2020; Statista, 2020a). Likewise, ecommerce platforms have seen a significant increase in digital footfall and sales as people are barred from high streets, supermarkets, and their normal shopping habits, which has meant increases in personal data and private information collection via cookies and other sales and marketing data (Office for National Statistics, 2020; Statista, 2020b).

As global populations retreated from offline social interactions both the use of data and shedding of personal data online have increased exponentially. For example, Virgin Media, a major UK internet service provider (ISP) with approximately 5.5 million customers, has reported that,

> network insights reveal how a 'new normal' has been established over the emergency period, during which Virgin Media customers have been using significantly more data. Since lockdown started, every Virgin Media broadband customer has downloaded an extra 3.4GB of data per day on average when compared with download levels in February – the month before lockdown measures began. That's enough additional usage for every customer to watch two films – or around 3.5 hours of Netflix video – every day, in addition to how they used their broadband before the emergency period. When it comes to upstream traffic – data sent by people while on video calls or sending emails – the relative change is even bigger. With more people remote working, gaming and socialising online, Virgin Media customers are now uploading an extra 3.7GB each week which is enough extra data for every customer to make 14 hours of 1-1 high-quality video calls on Zoom or send a staggering 185,000 emails.
>
> (2020)

To recall the hairy data analogy in the previous chapter, unable to go to the hairdresser and worried about hair maintenance, many people opted to shave their heads in lockdown (Harper, 2020). Likewise, prevented from their 'normal' social activities, many people have adopted a 'new normal' that includes shedding more personal data. Where we can no longer give of ourselves in public, we are giving of ourselves abundantly from the privacy and sanctity of our homes in the form of massive deluges of personal data. As we emerge slowly but surely from our homes and lockdown into the blindly and disorientating light of a post-Covid-19 world, one in which gregariousness and sociality have become potential sources of risk and threat, the intermingling of data as much as bodies is now of paramount concern. Data that stands apart from us as abstract Covid-19 statistics, and data that must speak us, perhaps even betrays us when it reveals behaviour and movement that run contrary to government guidance.

This is not the place to discuss or analyse in depth the full range of legal consequences and ramifications of Covid-19. Notwithstanding the extreme impact of the virus on social cohesion, organisation and governance in England (rules may differ in Scotland, Wales, and Northern Ireland), existing laws and regulations have addressed problems relating to or caused by the virus, including police powers to regulate and disperse crowds and issue fines to enforce social distancing rules (Metropolitan Police, 2020). These powers are, arguably, far beyond pre-Covid-19 powers, but they are not unfamiliar. However, the rules and the powers to enforce, for example social distancing, remain unfixed and subject to constant revision as the combination of science (public health) and politics (government) decide on how to manage the virus response. What we know is that new legislation, such as the UK *Coronavirus Act* 2020, mandates use of technologies, and videoconferencing in particular, in court proceedings as a specific response to social distancing rules (ss.535–7). Although, again, these technologies are not new in courts and for some commentators they were already key to the future of adjudication and justice (Susskind, 2019). But, like any other software or online-enabled technologies, data, and personal data in particular, are central to their operation. Therefore, a proliferation of online courts that combine case management, mediation, video and audio evidence gathering, and other key features of court proceedings will mean the production (the giving) of more personal data than it is possible to capture in offline courts. Managing and securing that data also becomes a greater burden (Magrath, 2018). When we read these changes back through the exemptions that General Data Protection Regulation (GDPR) offers for 'judicial independence and proceedings' and 'law enforcement purposes' then online justice becomes a site of significant data gathering potential that will only be exacerbated by social distancing rules that require digital justice as the 'new normal'.

Counting the peas ...

Watching the numbers of global infections and deaths rise has become part of the pandemic 'new normal'. Like the old man counting peas in Albert Camus' *The Plague*, the exercise has assumed an air of mechanical indifference: 'When Rieux entered the room, the old man was sitting up in bed, at his usual occupation, counting out dried peas from one pan to another' (1960, p. 58). Data dashboards built by the likes of Johns Hopkins University and the World Health Organization (WHO) provide a visualisation of the massive volumes of data collected around the world with aim to inform and provide knowledge on the virus, but arguably obscure its meaning and fail to relieve the sense of morbid tabulation. Millions of people have been and will be touched by the virus, either by contracting the virus, knowing of someone who does, or knowing someone who dies because of infection or complications related to Covid-19. We get some meaning of the effects of the virus at a personal level because of its impact on our lives, but data reflecting millions of infections and thousands of deaths across culturally and socioeconomically diverse nations is far harder to grasp or understand. Large numbers or complex mathematical models are rarely user friendly, hence the reason data visualisation has become popular and effective ways of showing general populations (who care to look) the impact of the virus globally. The risk, threat, danger, and warning of virus spread have become increasingly larger red dots hovering over regions and countries on a map, rather than increasingly larger numbers on a spreadsheet. Not born of any malicious intent, the result of the constant barrage of Covid-19 data, and the news that data generates, become emptied of real meaning other than the ability to fuel rational and irrational anxieties, anger, melancholy, and mourning for lost, pre-coronavirus ideals and freedoms.

As countries emerge from lockdowns and attempt to prevent further ones, many of the newly minted politico-scientific governance bodies and structures consider monitoring the transmission of the virus – which communities it moves through and why – a vital pre-vaccination and immunity strategy. But monitoring the virus is not only a health measure, in fact it is arguably a symptom of the relegation of health policies in favour of economic policies and, sometimes, political expediency. Chas Kissick *et al.* point out that monitoring, especially in the form of so-called contact tracing, is a 'technological intervention that seemed to have the potential to save lives while enabling a hamstrung economy to safely inch back open; it was a fixation of many public health and privacy advocates; it was the thing that was going to help us get out of this mess if we could manage the risks' (2020). The past tense of that statement is telling and reflects that the technological 'solutions' have yet to materialise in any meaningful way. But monitoring the virus by monitoring the virus' hosts, you and me, aims to unwind strict public health measure of lockdown and quarantine. This means easing the inherent risks and threats associated with airborne and aerosol pathogens that come from humans sharing the same air in confined spaces. Human gregariousness and sociality are, therefore, by extension the threat of upmost concern and the aim of monitoring the virus is to reassure and encourage people back into a (natural) state of gregariousness and sociality for the benefit, in the main, of the economic salvation of individuals, communities, and nations. It is an unenviable balancing act. As Jonathan Welburn of the US Rand Corporation maintains:

> We have a health crisis, we have an economic crisis, and together they're creating a national well-being crisis. Flattening the curve and not overwhelming the health system is something we've all

really accepted. But we also have to try not to overwhelm the economic system. We're trying to balance these two absolutely catastrophic and simultaneous crises.

(Rand, 2020)

Covid-19 has revealed in much starker detail because of its global effects the complex interlinking of health and economy and regional, national and international levels. 'The immense economic toll of the crisis also carries health risks', maintains Michael Boskin, because, 'Household financial stress tends to lead to increased substance abuse, domestic violence, and even suicide' (2020).

'Test and trace' and 'track and trace' are initiatives led by the National Health Service (NHS) and the hospitality sector in the United Kingdom (pubs, cafes, restaurants, etc.) forming part of the global 'exposure notification' response to Covid-19. Both systems monitor the spread of Covid-19 in domestic and regional populations using technologies such as smartphones applications ('apps') and non-digital methods such as a guest book or visitor record manual tracing. Whether digital, non-digital, or likely a combination of the two, exposure notification systems rely on intimate, connected, transient, and often fleeting social moments and encounters between individuals for identifying vectors in the virus's day-to-day transmission. Like a random selection of tourists on a tiny island in the Bay of Kotor, or the dried peas counted from one pan to another by the old man in *The Plague*, populations are isolated and read like a time and location stamped register of interconnected and interrelated beings. Whilst the 'analogue' practice of writing the name and contact details of customers is easily adopted by bars and restaurants and likely to be a more cost-effective option for many businesses (as the Information Commissioner's Office in the United Kingdom imply[1]), the efficacy of such an approach is questionable in larger and less easily controlled environments such as civic spaces or public transport systems. In these environments, smart phones exchange random numbers or 'keys' between phones using Bluetooth signals as they pass (like ships in the night), and the proximity of individuals determines the likelihood of contact with and transmission of the virus in the event a user of the contact tracing app reports infection.

The benefit of using Bluetooth is, arguably, because the system need not reveal details of the person, only an anonymous ID. This is a measure designed to protect privacy, as Google and Apple, working together on an exposure notification system, maintain.[2] Further, it is claimed that, 'Contact-tracing apps, while an effective method of combating the spread of COVID-19, have raised concerns about the use of technologies that could lead to the storing and sharing of sensitive personal data to identify infected individuals. Google and Apple's API is built to address those concerns, and to be sufficiently flexible to ensure it is compatible with the privacy requirements of different legislation' (Lexology, 2020a). At an individual level this is an interesting example of how proximate personal data, not the data subjects or ones to whom data relates, are objects of most interest. It is, to recall our earlier discussion, another example of the separation of data from subject, one in which the subject may become ill and die from coronavirus, but the data prevails as an echo of the moment of transmission and infection.

A major problem with contact tracing apps, even those that 'appear' on Google Android or Apple smartphones without being downloaded, is users must still voluntarily activate and consent to them, agreeing to 'buy into' and trust that the systems will not undermine their privacy by, for example, using collected data for purposes other than contact tracing. Notwithstanding the irony of a person who might take to Twitter or Facebook to protest the invasion of their privacy by an exposure notification app, as Jonathan Zittrain highlights limiting data collection to pseudonymous proximity could be a lost opportunity regarding valuable socio-medical data (2020). Zittrain argues that, 'the technology behind what have been variously called digital contact tracing or exposure notification tools could greatly inform and aid the traditional mechanisms of municipal health authorities' (2020). So, for example, 'map data could help contact tracers know whether an already-established proximate contact took place inside or outside, in a place with small rooms or large ones, in a dining establishment vs. an ER waiting room. The more data a health official has, the more a useful, artisanal judgment about contacts can be made' (Zittrain, 2020). Extending the potential reach of data collection in the name of fighting Covid-19 has come at an inopportune time for data privacy and protection advocates. GDPR and similar legislation are far from perfect, but they have moved the dial in terms of how we perceive the handling and management of data and sensitive information by governments and commercial actors. That it might undermine the forward momentum of tighter data privacy controls for the sake of the pandemic is not a straightforward decision, but yet another delicate balancing act. As discussed on the legal research site, *Lexology*,

The use of data is a critical tool in the fight against COVID-19. In some cases, this will necessarily involve the use of personal data, which relates to identified individuals and of course, due to the nature of the current crisis, sensitive health data. The UK data protection regulator, the ICO, has made it clear that data protection laws do not seek to prevent the use of data in order to combat the spread of this dreadful disease, but are intended to work in the public interest and enable health and safety to be prioritised where necessary. However, there remains a need to ensure that personal data is used in a proportionate manner with due respect to privacy rights, wherever possible.

(*Lexology,* 2020b)

Covid-19 has punctured the routine function, integrity, and normality of domestic and global governance and, importantly, the *datus quo* in ways one might only expect in the extremities of theory or thought experiments. Technologies and the use of personal and non-personal data feature in the answers to these questions, as we have seen. In an earlier chapter I raised the point of personal data anonymisation, and how data controllers use it to protect data subjects and often offer it as a concession when collecting extensive amounts of data. I argued that anonymisation is a logical conclusion in economic strategies of depersonalisation where it represents a willing commitment, by business, government and the data subject alike, to uncouple messy humanity from its valuable kernel. Anonymisation it now seems is a driving force behind exposure notification systems. These techniques provide succour to the data subject worried about threats to privacy, personal security, and so on. However, prophylactic measures such as anonymisation do not change the hunger for data, nor does it change the bonds and tensions necessary for government and business to build and maintain with individual and communities of data subjects. It may even encourage a greater extraction of personal data, and the hunger for personal data in the wake of Covid-19 may increase beyond levels anyone could have imagined. But, as so many like to say of the times we are living through, that would be another 'unprecedented' step among many.

Conclusion

It is worth admitting at this point that I did not expect to write this chapter. How could I have known that Covid-19 would bear down on the world and upend so much that humanity takes for granted? Even when I began writing this book in late January 2020 the virus was a vague news story from China. There were strong predictions that the local outbreak in Wuhan might spread further, but it was uncertain that it would reach pandemic levels, or that it would have such far-reaching global consequences in such a short space of time. As Graham Harman might say, the virus is not an object with definite or literal birth, maturation, and death points yet, so it is not possible to reflect or make definitive statements on it. This chapter was important to add because of the obvious role that technology and personal data are playing in managing the pandemic. But whilst questioning who the virus monitors are and what motivates them is important, it is neither a new nor radical enterprise. I have deliberately avoided commenting at length on debates regarding, what is perceived by some to be, privacy intrusions and restrictions on liberties because of Covid-19, which sparked protests in several countries in the spring of 2020. I do not disagree or dispute that certain technologies and personal data are well primed for the tasks of tracking, tracing, monitoring, and so on, and the technologies that emerge from this may yet prove to be the basis of a transformative political reality which many would like the present pandemic to create. The positive or negative effects of technology and personal data use concerning Covid-19 are not yet clear. A new horizon in the authority of personal data and the technological mechanisms to generate, create, sense, capture, and store it is just opening up, and there is no going back. Even as countries experiment with releasing and re-tightening social restrictions in a constant battle of attrition between public health and economy, and as the 'distant clamour of a populace rejoicing in its new-won freedom could be faintly heard', Camus' metaphor rings aloud, as the old fellow continues as usual; transposing peas from one pan to another (1960, p. 295).

Responses to the problems and the 'new normal' created by Covid-19 have meant an immediate pivot by societies to the assurances, utility, and range of personal devices (Bluetooth in smartphones, for example). More sophisticated systems, such as quantum computing, machine learning, artificial intelligence (AI), facial recognition, and algorithms to track and trace the virus are equally poised not to monitor the virus through physical populations *per se* but through past, present, and future populations of aggregated personal data. Debates have (re-)ignited between those who believe in unassailable rights to privacy that mitigate data extraction by government, and those who view restrictions on individual and civil liberties represented by a loosening of data protections a small price to pay for mastering and containing the virus. Despite the level of sophistication of the technologies used in the present moment compared with even recent systems for data capture and analysis, such as facial recognition software capable of identifying someone with a face mask, the debates and arguments concerning recent technological interventions are not new (Facewatch, 2020). In Chapter 1 I highlighted many of the same concerns raised by the public, politicians, lawyers, and academics with the rise of data banks.

But Covid-19 has also shone a light on the rampant dysfunctionality of hitherto stable liberal democracies. Society has not collapsed in countries such as the United Kingdom, Brazil, or the United States because of the pandemic, but the virus has shown contemporary capitalist societies are fragile and in many respects ill-equipped to cope with jarring and radical shifts from norms that capitalism establishes to maintain and support itself; norms that have, for at least forty years, been developed using data. Businesses, large and small, forecast difficult years ahead as they run out of cash and face government bailouts, furlough schemes, and loan expiry that many will struggle to repay either in the coming year or at all. Small business and entrepreneurial trends so often lauded as ground-breaking, agile, and innovative, and large corporations have all, it now seems, been taking on excessive risks and operating at the very margins of economic sustainability and feasibility. Many have insufficient or non-existent financial safety-nets, little or no cash in the bank, and have resorted to mass redundancies in numbers not seen for many generations. Also, the beating hearts of contemporary capitalist societies, the markets, cannot solve global uncertainty caused by the virus and are instead rising and falling and in ways which seem more detached from reality than usual. Markets are, should it not have been clear before Covid-19 pulled back the curtain to reveal the stark truth, a dangerous fantasyland. Ideologically the virus has upended things. The pandemic has revealed inherent and often extreme vulnerabilities in national administrative infrastructures and the global economic system alike. Right-wing governments around the world are turning to measures including the nationalisation of industries, which implies a belief that free-market competitive capitalism might suit good times, but socialism works.

At a fundamental level capitalism cannot cope with, what we may call, an 'anthropause'. It desperately needs labour to produce surplus value, to maintain growth and stave off contraction. Lockdown and quarantine are economically catastrophic primarily because they cut off labour, much like a strike does. But not labour in terms of data production, and that could well be the lifeline that capitalism needs. We should view data labour from different angles, some of benefit to capitalism, others far less so as they are informed by socialist, cooperative, and unionising positions and rhetoric. In terms of the *datus quo*, the way data labour presently looks is a boon for capitalism, and as a response to economic fall-back because of Covid-19, capitalism will want to preserve that position. This is because data labour, especially in terms of social media and ecommerce platforms, involves a great deal of data production by users, subscribers, customers, and so on, but with little or no compensation. 'Most people', Eric Posner and E. Glen Weyl point out, 'do not realize the extent to which their labor – as data producers – powers the digital economy' (2018, p. 208). On this matter I agree with Posner and Weyl, as earlier chapters in this book will attest. But I do not agree with their solution – one equally shared by Jaron Lanier (2014) – which is for greater market intervention and proliferation, albeit under the rubric of 'radical markets'.

I am hesitant about this position is because of the clear neoliberal overtones. Like the promise of data sovereignty, the vision of data labour (or 'data work') set out by Posner and Weyl does not only unlock an individual's potential sovereign wealth. That is, money (fiat currency, tokens, or cryptocurrency) an individual might hope to make from their data-to-day online activities, such as micro-payments that accrue from the use and sale of personal data to platforms instead of having it taken and used without renumeration. What accompanies this data sovereignty and data labour is an individual's stake in the effective operation of various markets and economies, meaning that will have to work constantly, diligently, and efficiently to ensure micro- and macro-data economies thrive. As Marx and many other critics of capitalism and political economy tell us, this leads to the rationalisation of human reason in harmony with money and markets. Data labour, much like earlier industrial forms of work, is an invention of the so-called fourth industrial revolution, our current stage of capitalism hungry for information, innovative technologies, and, above all, data. I would argue that there are several strategies used in earlier forms of industrialisation that are just as if not more effective today because they relied upon the scientific organisation of labour that information technologies and data production today achieve so well. 'The economic rationalization of labour did not consist merely in making pre-existent productive activities more methodical and better adapted to their object', argues André Gorz of the strategies of the first industrial age,

> It was a revolution, a subversion of the way of life, the values, the social relations and relation to Nature, the *invention* in the full sense of the word of something which had never existed before. Productive activity was cut off from its meaning, its motivations and its object and became simply a *means* of earning a wage. It ceased to be part of life and became the *means* of 'earning a

living'. Time for working and time for living became disjointed; labour, its tools, its products acquired a reality distinct from that of the worker and were governed by decisions taken by someone else the satisfaction of 'producing works' together and the pleasure derived from 'doing' were abolished in favour of only those satisfactions that money could buy.

(1989, pp. 21–22)

Gorz's description of the first brutal effects of capitalism in the nineteenth century is now so engrained in the fabric of today's society that we barely register them any longer. Economic rationalisation has triumphed. With data labour we are starting from a point of utter surrender to forms of productive activity on- and offline that we are told, and believe to our very core, must pay. This is not an argument in contradiction to the role of GDPR in securing greater rights for data subjects, nor, therefore, one in favour of the pendulum swinging back towards gratuitous exploitation. It is an argument aimed at the complacency of viewing 'data work' as a means to an end *qua* financial reward. Compensation or remuneration for data work may appear equitable responses to the exploitation and abuses of platform capitalism in recent years, therefore, but it cannot and should not be a long-term option. It will only give capitalism the fuel and the raw material it so desperately wants: data.

Notes

1. https://ico.org.uk/global/data-protection-and-coronavirus-information-hub/contact-tracing-protecting-customer-and-visitor-details/ (accessed 29 July 2020)
2. https://www.google.com/covid19/exposurenotifications/ (accessed 29 July 2020)

References

Balancing Public Health and Economic Effects of Physical Distancing: Q&A with Jonathan Welburn. 2020. *Rand Review*, 13 July. https://www.rand.org/blog/rand-review/2020/07/balancing-public-health-and-economic-effects.html (accessed 30 July 2020).

Coronavirus Impact on Retail e-Commerce Website Traffic Worldwide as of March 2020b. *Statista*, 17 July. https://www.statista.com/statistics/1112595/covid-19-impact-retail-e-commerce-site-traffic-global/ (accessed 28 July 2020).

COVID-19: Data Protection Lessons from Google's Contact-tracing API. 2020a. *Lexology*, 7 July. https://www.lexology.com/library/detail.aspx?g=21679085-cbe5-4c3e-b6de-fa255f3e5828 (accessed 30 July 2020).

Data Privacy & COVID-19 in the UK: Q&A on Key Privacy Issues. 2020b. *Lexology*, 4 May. https://www.lexology.com/library/detail.aspx?g=42855031-262e-4b59-845f-321a31b92d22 (accessed 30 July 2020).

Facewatch Launches Facemask Recognition Upgrade. 2020. *Facewatch*, 11 May. https://www.facewatch.co.uk/2020/05/11/facewatch-launches-facemask-recognition-upgrade/ (accessed 13 May 2020).

In-home Media Consumption due to the Coronavirus Outbreak Among Internet Users Worldwide as of March 2020, by Country. 2020a. *Statista*, 18 June. https://www.statista.com/statistics/1106498/home-media-consumption-coronavirus-worldwide-by-country/ (accessed 28 July 2020).

Retail Sales, Great Britain: June 2020. 2020. *Office for National Statistics*, 24 July. https://www.ons.gov.uk/businessindustryandtrade/retailindustry/bulletins/retailsales/june2020 (accessed 28 July 2020).

Social Distancing Rules During Coronavirus in England. 2020. *Metropolitan Police*. https://www.met.police.uk/advice/advice-and-information/c19/coronavirus-covid-19/coronavirus-social-distancing-rules-england/ (accessed 29 July 2020).

Virgin Media Reveals Extent of Lockdown Leap in Broadband Traffic Growth. 2020. *Virgin Media*, 17 June. https://www.virginmedia.com/corporate/media-centre/press-releases/virgin-media-reveals-extent-of-lockdown-leap-in-broadband-traffic-growth (accessed 29 July 2020).

Bell, Genevieve. 2020. The Benevolent Panopticon. *MIT Technology Review*. Vol. 123, No. 3, pp. 16–19.

Boskin, Michael. 2020. Economic Recovery from the Covid-19 Crisis Will Need a Balancing Act. *The Guardian*, 28 April. https://www.theguardian.com/business/2020/apr/28/economic-recovery-covid-19-crisis-politics (accessed 30 July 2020).

Camus, Albert. 1960. *The Plague*. Translated by Stuart Gilbert. London: Penguin.

Gibney, Elizabeth. 2020. Coronavirus Lockdowns Have Changed the Way Earth Moves. *Nature*, 31 March. https://www.nature.com/articles/d41586-020-00965-x (accessed 29 July 2020).

Gorz, André. 1989. *Critique of Economic Reason*. London: Verso.

Harper, Leah. 2020. Shave It or Save It? The 11 Big Lockdown Hair Conundrums – Answered by Experts. *The Guardian*, 28 April. https://www.theguardian.com/fashion/2020/apr/28/shave-it-or-save-it-the-11-big-lockdown-hair-conundrums-answered-by-experts (accessed 29 July 2020).

He, Guojun, Yuhang Pan and Takanao Tanaka. 2020. The Short-Term Impacts of COVID-19 Lockdown on Urban Air Pollution in China. *Nature Sustainability*. https://www.nature.com/articles/s41893-020-0581-y#citeas (accessed 29 July 2020).

Jackson, Mark. 2020. COVID-19 – EE Report Reveals Internet Traffic During Lockdown. *ISPreview*, 26 May. https://www.ispreview.co.uk/index.php/2020/05/covid-19-ee-report-reveals-internet-traffic-during-lockdown.html (accessed 28 July 2020).

Kissick, Chas, Elliot Setzer and Jacob Schulz. 2020. What Ever Happened to Digital Contact Tracing? *Law Fare*, 21 July. https://www.lawfareblog.com/what-ever-happened-digital-contact-tracing (accessed 29 July 2020).

Lanier, Jaron. 2014. *Who Owns the Future?* London: Penguin.

Magrath, Paul. 2018. Transparency, Data Protection and the Law Courts of the Future. *Legal Information Management*. Vol. 18, No. 2, pp. 70–75.

Poe, Edgar Allen. 1998. *Selected Tales*. Edited by David Van Leer. Oxford: Oxford World Classics.

Posner, Eric and E. Glen Weyl. 2018. *Radical Markets: Uprooting Capitalism and Democracy for a Just Society*. Princeton: Princeton University Press.

Rae, Gavin. 2012. Being and Technology: Heidegger on the Overcoming of Metaphysics. *Journal of the British Society of Phenomenology*. Vol. 43, No. 3, pp. 305–325.

Susskind, Richard. 2019. *Online Courts and the Future of Justice*. Oxford: Oxford University Press.

Zittrain, Jonathan. 2020. Entering the Minefield of Digital Contact Tracing. *Medium*, 5 May. https://medium.com/berkman-klein-center/entering-the-minefield-of-digital-contact-tracing-9c042941bb23 (accessed 29 July 2020).

Index

Printed in the United States
by Baker & Taylor Publisher Services